HOME OFFICE DESIGN

HOME OFFICE DESIGN

EVERYTHING YOU NEED TO KNOW ABOUT PLANNING,
ORGANIZING, AND FURNISHING YOUR WORK SPACE

Neal Zimmerman, AIA

JOHN WILEY & SONS, INC.
New York ▪ Chichester ▪ Brisbane ▪ Toronto ▪ Singapore

Library of Congress Cataloging-in-Publication Data
Zimmerman, Neal.
    Home office design : everything you need to know about planning, organizing, and furnishing your work space / Neal Zimmerman.
        p.   cm.
    ISBN 0-471-13433-3 (paper : alk. paper)
    1. Office decoration.   I. Title.
NK2195.04Z56   1996
    725'.23—dc20   96-17528

Printed in the United States of America

10   9   8   7   6   5   4   3   2   1

CONTENTS

PREFACE

IN RECENT YEARS, THE INTRODUCTION of low-cost computer systems, communications equipment, and services has made it possible to set up a main or alternate work location at home. At the same time, economic, social, and environmental factors have converged to make the idea of working at home more attractive to consultants, employers, and employees alike. Estimates of the number of people working at home, either full or part time, currently run as high as 40 million, and that figure is growing rapidly.

When a workforce is centralized, the cost of hiring design professionals to plan office space is justified by economies of scale. Smaller companies that rent space in a speculative office building are usually provided with planning assistance as part of the lease.

In contrast, the vast majority of home office workers do not have access to professional design assistance, though the physical organization of their work environment at home is as important as it was in the office. Many corporate telecommuters, who are the fastest growing segment of all home-workers, are provided with surprisingly little guidance or support to help them organize their physical work environment at home. Because the home office boom developed recently and rapidly, and because people are being dispersed one at a time, into a broad variety of environments, there are few standards or resources available to help them organize and plan their home offices. They are often left to "fly by the seat of their pants."

Without any prior experience, many home office workers are single-handedly faced with the task of turning space that was intended for living into office use, while simultaneously integrating a working office into their existing living environment.

The results are typically far from glamorous. Homeworkers often begin with limited equipment in a makeshift location in an apartment or house, perhaps even on a kitchen table or, more commonly, at a desk in a bedroom or a den. As needs arise, they improvise. When the arrangement proves to be ongoing and viable, they contemplate a higher level of organization and a dedication of space.

Although there have been a number of books written on the business aspects of working at home, such as marketing, finance, and time management, there is very little information available about planning or designing a home office.

For the myriad people who are unable to find information, advice, examples, and resources, *Home Office Design* seeks to be a remedy. *Home Office Design* will help individuals who are contemplating the design or redesign of a home office to visualize some of the possibilities, to become acquainted with issues that involve planning and to gather ideas or inspiration from presented examples. It may also serve as a general overview and resource guide for design professionals.

Although electronic technology is critical to home office activity, it is actually becoming easier to incorporate it into the home environment. Newer systems are smaller, multifunctional, and simplified, requiring less space, power, and protection than systems of the very recent past. In many aspects, the equipment has become somewhat less demanding and less vulnerable.

As a result, home office design is driven less by the requirements for equipment. This gives us more freedom to concentrate on issues such as spatial separation, functional utility, commodiousness, productivity, comfort, enjoyment of the work space, and harmony with the overall life space. Lifestyle enhancement can and should be one of the major benefits of working at home.

Having a well-organized home office doesn't mean that you have to spend a fortune. Whether you are working in a one-room apartment, or whether you plan on building an addition to your home, the principles of organization remain the same. There are usually a number of ways to solve a problem—one of which will suit your requirements and budget.

It is my opinion that the heart of any working office is the "workstation." By this I mean the place where you process and communicate your words and ideas. Without a comfortable, properly equipped, and well-organized workstation, you will struggle to be productive and you may jeopardize success.

Fortunately, several manufacturers have recently introduced products that have been expressly developed for home offices. Other products work equally well in a home office or a corporate setting. I have included a broad array of these products, focusing on their beneficial features. There are representative products from every price range for desks, computer workstations, "offices-in-a-closet," storage systems, seating, paper organization, and accessories. Some products, especially workstations, are sold "ready-to-assemble," which enables the manufacturers to control their production and shipping costs. The savings are passed on to you. Assembly at home is usually very simple and quick.

For those of you who are considering renovating a portion of your home, building an addition, or a new house with a home office, we've covered the basic planning concepts for these kinds of projects as they relate to home office design. Also, we have included some fine examples. It is my feeling that if you are going this route, you should seek the help of a local design professional. I encourage you to do so. My intentions are to give you the "lay of the land," and to help you become a better educated client.

A substantial and growing number of corporate employees are now working at home, either part-, or full-time. This trend is simultaneously influencing corporate office design, which is about to undergo the most radical transformation since the advent of open-office planning, a generation ago.

Finally, one of the most interesting new developments is again a technological one: the introduction of low-cost networked desktop video communication. We are now able to log onto a system that enables us to call and see each other on-screen. As costs continue to drop, desktop video is destined to become as commonplace as the car telephone. This technology, which emulates face-to-face contact, will ease the feeling of isolation caused by working in a remote location.

In the last 150 years, there have been three major shifts in how and where we work to earn a living. We are on the forefront of a new age of work organization, it is certain. And with anything new, there is often a painful learning curve. I hope that this book eases the curve, and helps to make working at home more comfortable, more productive, and more pleasurable, as we learn to adjust to one of the many by-product changes of the information era.

Neal Zimmerman
June 1996

ACKNOWLEDGMENTS

FIRST, THANKS GO TO Chuck Pinckney and Izzy Gesell, who inadvertently planted the seeds that grew into this book.

Thanks also to friends and experienced authors themselves, who steered me through the proposal process: Ken (Lazlo) Haas, Jackie (Mrs. Elite) Costello, and Paul Tieger, Member of the Royal Order.

Then there were the many friends who contributed suggestions and encouragement: Jeff "Dr. B" Bianco, Sid Blumenthal, Roger Gohl, Jacqueline Hamilton, Norman Katz (Burgermeister), Leonard Lang, Jim Laser, Rick Lavigne, Magnus Magnusson, Don Meixner, Brad Mellor, Joanne Pratt, Bob Rogers, Don Sachar, Howard Schachter, Roger Spears, Larry Tattenbaum, and David Trowbridge.

Research on the project was made easy for me by Judy (Info-Queen) Eisenberg at the West Hartford Connecticut Public Library; and the *info*mous Dennis (the One and Only) Geller, who has been very generous with his time and counsel.

Several individuals helped form the content and direction of the book. I especially wish to thank the following:

Jean Davenport	*SNET*
Michael Dodson	*Digital Equipment Corporation*
Don Dotter	*Ergometrix*
Tina Facos-Casolo	*IBM*
Dan Flohr	*Target Technologies*
Don Griesdorn	*BKM Total Office*
Jeff Hallett	*PresentFutures Group*

Carl Kirkpatrick   *J.C. Penney Company*
Jim McGarry   *Business Products Industry Association*
Sally O'Malley   *Pacific Design Center*
Karen Odlum   *Aetna Companies*
Gene Quaglia   *Intel*
Mark Regulinksi   *Skidmore, Owings & Merrill Architects*
Mark Schurman   *Herman Miller, Inc.*
Chuck Searle   *Staples, Inc.*
Lou Slawetsky   *Industry Analysts, Inc.*
Beverley Williams   *National Association of
                         Home-Based Businesses*

Thank you also to John Ray Hoke at AIA headquarters, Patricia Beatty at ASID headquarters, Judy Edwards at the AIA/Connecticut chapter, and the directors of over forty components of the American Society of Interior Designers, and the American Institute of Architects, for helping me to acquire some excellent photo examples of home office design.

My hat is off to Amanda Miller, Editor at John Wiley & Sons, as well as her assistant MaryAlice Yates, for their attention, direction, and hand-holding during the many months of researching, writing, organizing and fretting.

Finally, I want to thank my son Jon Zimmerman (who proofread portions of the text), my steadfast parents Rose and Richard Zimmerman, and my loving partner Leann Sherman, whose patience, love, and support have enabled me to embark upon and complete this voyage.

HOW TO USE THIS BOOK

IF YOU ARE PLANNING A HOME OFFICE for the first time, I suggest that you carefully read the first few chapters to gain an overview of the concepts involved in organizing an area in your home for work. The chapters build upon each other, starting with concepts and eventually getting down to the "nuts-and-bolts." I also recommend that you underline the items or ideas that you think will be applicable to your situation, so that you can quickly refer back to them.

Organizing and Budgeting

The book includes a number of inventory sheets that will help you to maintain control (and sanity) as you organize your working environment at home. Photocopy these sheets and staple them together, so that you can make notes on them freely. You can recopy the originals if you need fresh blanks.

Make a list of the information you will need, people you wish to speak with, and purchases you will need to make. Start making a preliminary budget as quickly as you can. Sample budget forms and lists of typical equipment are included to make the job easier for you.

Although some of the home office examples and products presented in this book may reach beyond your budget, I have also included several unique and cost-conscious solutions to typical home office design problems. Organization and functional utility don't necessarily have to be gilt-edged, or expensive.

Examples   You will see several drawings depicting typical workstation arrangements and room layouts, both in two and three dimensions. You should be able to find a layout that has some similarities with a location that you may be considering for your home office.

Furniture   In preparing this book, I researched the marketplace for
and   companies that are making furniture and work tools suit-
Ergonomic   able for the home office environment. I was amazed to find
Equipment   a large number of companies who have targeted their efforts to the home office market, and who are providing innovative solutions at many different price ranges. No matter what your setup, I'm sure that you will find ideas and products that will help you to create an excellent home office environment.

Picking a place to "set up shop" in your home may become a balancing act. Chapter 2, Choosing a Work Space Location in the Home Office, should help you make an educated decision.

Your personal workstation is where you will spend most of your time. Chapter 3, Planning for Workstations, will help you to determine size, configuration, and other workstation needs.

Now you can get down to measured planning, which will be explained in Chapter 5, Puttin' it All Together. You can do this with rough sketches on graph paper,[1] or if you are so inclined, you can use a computer-design program. The program presented in this book is simple enough for a nonprofessional to learn and use quickly. It has a library of home and office furniture, which you can drop right into your floor plan.

Some furniture dealers may be able to provide you with planning assistance; if you bring a floor plan to them, with

---

1 Right about now, you may be saying to yourself, "Me, draw? He's got to be kidding!" I don't want to scare you, and I certainly don't expect you to become a professional drafter overnight. Only the simplest "layout" drawings are needed, and you can do the job on graph paper, with a pencil and a six-inch ruler. Directions will show you how. But by all (or any) means, get something down on paper. You'll have all your information in one place, and you will be able to explain what you need to others as the planning develops. You will also know what fits before you start moving in furniture.

ideas about what you need and prefer, it will be easier for them to help you, and you will get better results.

Remember that planning a home office involves more than fitting furniture into a room. There are lighting, electrical, and ventilation issues to consider as well. These concerns may affect your location selection, and you may have to budget for a circuit, an air conditioning unit, or some overhead lighting, depending upon your specific environment. For help, read: Chapter 1, Home Office Planning "101"; Chapter 13, Renovations, Additions, and New Construction; and Chapter 4, Electrical Power Requirements.

With a budget and a plan, you're halfway there! Now comes the fun part, which is selecting furniture and equipment for the office. Items presented in this book are credited to their manufacturers or suppliers. Because prices are so variable, a graphic scale is presented below many captions to give you a sense of price range. You will have to call the manufacturers or dealers for current pricing. A list of them is provided at the back of the book.

For the Interior Designer or Architect

If you are preparing a project that involves a home office, *Home Office Design* will give you a quick overview of current thinking and basic planning issues and provide resource information for you. Source addresses are listed for furniture and equipment, and costs are comparatively ranged.

Renovations, Additions, and New Construction

Renovations, and especially additions are projects all by themselves; a home office addition is a project within a project. If you are contemplating a major home renovation, an addition for home office use, or a home office within brand new home, you are embarking on a project in two parts.

The first part is to plan the work environment, its size, organization, and equipment. Chapters 1 and 3 will help you to determine space requirements and functional relationships, which will have an impact on the size and location of your renovation or addition. Information on furniture and equipment will help you to plan and equip the work space, as well as arrive at a budget.

The second part of the project is to plan the office into the renovation, addition, or new home. Chapter 13 will give you an overview of the process, especially if this is your first project. You can begin thinking, inquiring, and educating yourself before you start spending money.

I firmly believe that you will save time and get better value for your money if you hire a local licensed design professional to help you get the job done. This person is still going to need your guidance. If you know your office needs, and a little bit about the process, you will achieve the best results.

Permits to Work at Home

Before beginning any home office project, be sure that local authorities will permit you to do so. (See page 172—Planning and Zoning Issues.)

Measure Twice— Cut Once!

This is an old saying in the building industry and it is well worth repeating. If you are careful in the planning stage, you will save time and money in the building stage. If you plan your office well, it will be a source of enjoyment for many years, and best of all, you will like "arriving at the office" each morning.

CHAPTER ONE
HOME OFFICE PLANNING "101"

Configuration from the JB Collection.

Courtesy of Herman Miller for the Home, Zeeland, MI. Photo by Nick Merrick, © Hedrich-Blessing.

WORKING OUT OF YOUR HOME is going to require that you balance your home life and work life in close proximity to each other. The location and organization of an office can be a tremendous help, or a hindrance to keeping you focused. It can be the difference between the success or failure of your home office as a productive workplace for you; and it may also determine the success or failure of a new business venture, or a telecommuting job.

What Is an Office?

My definition of an "office" is: a workplace where ideas are developed, recorded, and communicated. In this sense, a car or airplane seat could serve as an office, and indeed they sometimes do!

In essence, an office is a place where ideas are produced.

This definition distinguishes it from other workplaces such as farms, factories, workshops, or other production facilities, where *things* are produced. An office is an idea factory.

I like to think of an office as a working machine with a number of interrelated components, just like a car. After reviewing the basic components in this chapter, I think you will find that your home office will contain many of the features of a traditional office in a commercial building. It is likely, however, that space or amenities in your home will serve double duty. Space may have to be shared for both home and office use, or it may have to be "converted" from home to office, and vice versa, during the course of a single day.

In order to better visualize the relationships between components, take a look at Figure 1-1. We'll examine these components in detail in later chapters. For now, let's look at them conceptually, and see how they relate to each other.

Production Area

As you can see in the figure, three elements form the core of a working office, the area where work actually gets produced, or put another way, where "production" happens.

Work Space

The heart of the production area is the work space, the nerve center of business activity. This is the place where work gets done, where the "rubber meets the road," continuing with my car analogy. It is also where people typically spend most of their time while in the office. In a traditional

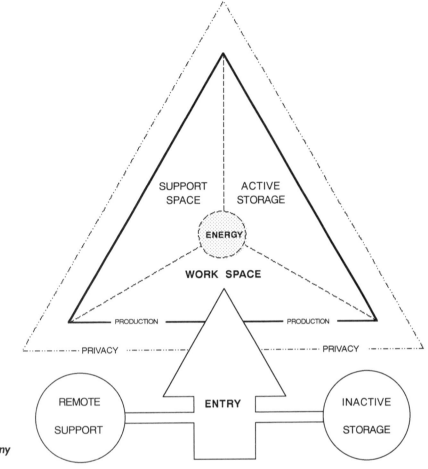

SUPPORT
SPACE

ACTIVE
STORAGE

ENERGY

WORK SPACE

PRODUCTION

PRODUCTION

PRIVACY

PRIVACY

REMOTE

SUPPORT

ENTRY

INACTIVE

STORAGE

Figure 1-1
Basic elements of any
working office.

office setting, everybody from the newest recruit to the chief executive officer has "turf" in the work space.[1] Another name for individual turf is the "workstation."

In a home office, the entire work space may consist of only one workstation. At its simplest, a workstation consists of a work surface and a seat. Most kinds of work in the information era require far more than this simple arrangement. Depending on the task(s) performed, space, equipment, and furnishing requirements for a workstation will vary.

Even if you plan to work at home alone, you may find that you will need more than one workstation in your work

1 In the traditional office, an employee's turf was permanent. Now, personal employee work space is often shared, or temporarily assigned.

space, or a way in which one workstation can support more than one function.

Workstation organization is so critical to the success of a working office that we have devoted two chapters to the subject (see Chapter 3, Planning Workstations and Chapter 7, Workstation Furniture).

Support Space
In contrast with work space, which is made up of workstations that are typically dedicated to the use of one individual, support spaces in a traditional office are usually shared. The traditional names for these spaces are conference room, reception area, mail room, library, and so on. In a home office, support space may have to be located in a location separate from the work space, although some convenience is sacrificed. If you are working solo and you don't expect to host visitors, your support space may wind up being integrated into a single workstation.

Active Storage
There are two basic kinds of storage: records and supplies. I am not including things that you may sell as part of supplies. If you provide goods as part of your business, you may need a warehouse, which could be anything from your garage to a special facility miles from your home.

Active storage is the stuff you use on a daily basis. Examples are active job files, current research materials, and office supplies that are consumed regularly, such as stationery, pens, and paper.

Some records and supplies need to be stored directly at the workstation; others may be stored in nearby storage spaces. The location of storage and the selection of appropriate storage containers will make a major difference in the appearance, efficiency and comfort of your office (see Chapter 9, Organizing, Filing, and Storage).

Energy
The things that you do, the equipment you use, and the nature of your home environment will all play a part in determining requirements for energy. Every office, whether it is a home office or a commercial office, will have to satisfy energy requirements in order to operate. This energy is delivered in four forms: light, power (electric and communications), climate control, and water.

1. Light

In most commercial offices, artificial light is used to illuminate all areas of the workplace. Overhead lights (most commonly, ceiling-mounted recessed fluorescent fixtures) are on whenever people are in the office. Windows are more prized for their view than they are for the light they provide. Indeed, many spaces in contemporary offices have no windows at all. In most modern office buildings, windows are intentionally fixed (i.e., they can't be opened) so as not to disturb the mechanical climate control system.

Even if you do have windows in your home office, you will still require artificial light. In fact, sunlight flooding into your office can create lighting problems, and also produce uncomfortable heat.

2. Electrical Power

In the good old days (we're talkin' yesteryear), offices ran just fine without electricity, thank you. Thomas Edison and the industrial revolution changed all that. Now almost every piece of office equipment needs electricity to operate, down to the stapler and pencil sharpener.

Once you start counting, you may be surprised at the total number of items you intend to plug into electrical outlets, including computer(s), copier, fax, modem, radio, lights, battery rechargers, docking equipment, and so on.

Each piece of equipment, every light bulb, and each person in your office will generate a certain amount of heat, and the cumulative effects may require supplementary air conditioning, requiring yet additional power. The reverse may also be true: because of climate and location in the home, supplementary heat may be required, which may also demand additional electric power.

Beyond the number of outlets, the number of circuits and the quality of the power are equally Important.(see Chapter 4, Electrical Power Requirements).

3. Communications Power

Most home office management experts agree that you should have a business telephone line separate from your personal line, especially if you have a family. Although it may seem simple at first, the arrangement that you make with the phone service company, and how you organize wiring in your office can get tricky. Your answering machine, computer, modem, fax machine, or copier may be tied to the communication loop.

4. Temperature Control

Depending upon your geographic climate, and the specifics of your home environment, you may have to provide additional heating and/or cooling. This will be especially true if you reclaim uninsulated garage, basement, or attic space. Heat generated by your equipment will have to be considered.

5. Water

Most core spaces will not require water, although it may be necessary for graphic artists, as an example, to have a cleanup sink in or very near their production area.

6. Refreshment and Restroom

If you receive no visitors, these peripheral support spaces are simply the house kitchen and the nearest bathroom. Employees and clients complicate matters. Both expect higher levels of separation between home and office use, as a matter of propriety.

Privacy and Separation

It is here that the home office contrasts most with the commercial office. In a traditional office building, a business usually has its own entry door, which is located off either private or shared lobby/hallway space. There is normally a complete physical separation between one business entity and another—businesses are separated from each other by full-height walls.

The purpose of the separation is to provide a focused and environmentally stabilized environment, so that individuals and groups can perform work tasks effectively. In a home office, the separations are often not as well-defined.

In a home office, the separation between work space and lifespace is often blended. The front entrance of the home office may also be the front entrance of the house or apartment. The office itself may be in a family room, or bedroom. This overlapping situation has implications for employees, clients, office organization, and work productivity.

Make no mistake about it: your home office will work only if you can "privatize" it when you are working, and protect it when you are away.

Personal Discipline

Ultimately, it will be your own personal discipline that keeps you at task, and away from the TV or the refrigerator during working hours. For instance, I make it a rule never to turn on my desk radio before noon. For me, radio is a distraction, and this system works for me.

From a design standpoint, the old adage "out-of-sight, out-of mind" helps to reduce temptation. It is best to locate your office away from distractions, or at least screened from them. If the line of sight from your workstation leads directly to your TV, as an example, it may trigger an urge to turn it on. Keep distractions out of sight, and make personal rules that you endeavor not to break.

Your home office should have boundaries, and the ability to control visual distractions (such as family member activities) or sound distractions (children playing, or stereos blaring) while you are conducting business. Some of these boundaries may be "political" rather than physical: that is to say, those who live with you know to keep themselves and other intrusions they create out of the way of the family room, when you are using it as an office.

The location you choose, how you arrange it, what you put in it, and the rules you make, can all affect the quality of privacy and separation, even if you are working in a shared space.

Entry

"Entry" is the element that breaches the separation, by connecting the core of operation of a working office with the outside world.

The ideal office has a private entry, which is a door from a public area directly into dedicated office space. Most home-offices will not have a private entry.

If you are working alone, and if you never have business visitors, the entry becomes less formal. In this case, "entry" is about separation—office versus living space. Entry may simply be a folding screen, or a part of a room which is off-limits to the family when you are working. It may even be a closeted office (see Chapters 3 and 7).

If you expect to have employees or clients in your home office, the consideration of entry becomes more formal and may involve a waiting area, as well as adjacencies to support space. Entry issues may predetermine where you locate your office within your home (see Chapter 2, Choosing a Workspace Location in the Home Office), or prompt you to consider making arrangements for off-site conferencing space.

Remote Support

Conferencing

It is possible to have a conference room in a home office that is moderately distant from the core production area. For instance, let's say you have a two-story home and you plan to work in the second floor bedroom, but you may occasionally host clients.

You might be able to solve your problem by "borrowing" a ground floor dining room, preferably near the front entry, for an occasional conference. In this case your client would not be invited into the production area. You should make every attempt, however, not to bring your clients through living space to gain access to other spaces that are used for work. It is not good business to publicly ignore the cultural conventions of work and home separation.

The above example could work in a high-rise apartment, as well as a two-story home, as long as the conventions are respected.

It may also be possible to rent off-site conferencing space not too far from your home office. If your home supports everything but your need for an occasional client conference, you may be able to make arrangements for conferencing support with a company that rents temporary office space on an hourly or daily basis.

Inactive Storage

Inactive storage may be located outside the core of operation. This kind of storage includes records of past or dormant projects. It also includes equipment that is not in use, and supplies that were bought in quantity. Tight quarters may force you to seek rental storage space for dormant storage.

Some people refer to inactive storage as "dead" storage. I say if storage is truly dead, bury it. You should review and selectively prune your inactive files every year, and your active files every six months. Through this process, you will also remember what you are storing, and how to get at it quickly.

Storage in an off-site location is difficult to access quickly. It is also an additional cost, which you may be able to eliminate by keeping storage volume to a minimum.

Basic Elements Checklist

In order to keep track of the parts and pieces of home office planning discussed so far, Figure 1-2 on the next page provides a basic elements checklist. It is a way of doing a preliminary planning inventory on one page. You can check off the elements that apply to you, and then focus in on them in later chapters.

The Benefits of Basic Planning

It's a "must" to have a sense of the basic requirements of operation, before you begin to choose a location for setting up an office in your home. The arrangement of a home office that is best for you will depend upon the kind of work you do, the characteristics of your domicile, your family arrangement, and your financial situation. If you set up in the wrong place, it may be hard to make a correction. If your are operating a home-based business, a poorly conceived work space can affect profitability, and cost you clients. Relocation can be expensive and time consuming.

That's All There Is

For a novice office planner, all these parts and pieces may seem overwhelming, at first. If you are planning to work at home, you will be faced with almost every issue raised. The good news is that if you have a general understanding of the basic planning elements, you will avoid a false start. Whatever your circumstances, the basic elements remain the same.

Now you are ready to think about choosing an appropriate location in your home to set up your home office.

COMPONENT		REQUIREMENT	Y/N		COMMENTS
WORK SPACE		COMPUTER			
		ADMINISTRATIVE			
		MEETING			
		PROJECT			
		EMPLOYEES			
SUPPORT		INTERVIEW/CLIENT MEETING			
		CONFERENCE			
		PRESENTATION			
		SPECIAL NEEDS			
STORAGE		JOB FILES			
		COMPUTER DISKS			
		BOOKS/MAGS/DIRECTORIES			
		STATIONERY			
		GENERAL OFFICE SUPPLIES			
ENERGY		LIGHT			
		ELECTRICAL POWER			
		TELECOMMUNICATIONS			
		TEMPERATURE CONTROL			
		WATER			
		REST/REFRESH			
PRIVACY		VISUAL			
		SOUND			
		SECURITY			
ENTRY		VISITORS			
REMOTE SUPPORT		CONFERENCE			
INACTIVE STORAGE		FILES			
		STOCK SUPPLIES			

Figure 1-2
Basic elements checklist.

CHAPTER TWO
CHOOSING A WORK SPACE LOCATION IN THE HOME OFFICE

Kendall Valley Series.
Courtesy of Sauder Woodworking, Archbold, OH.

A S WE HAVE SEEN IN THE CHAPTER on basic office planning, choosing a location in your home to set up a home office is a matter of balancing your work needs with requirements for privacy, access, energy, and available space.

Financial Priorities and Home Office Design

Many home office businesses are started with limited cash reserves, meaning that the owner (you) can finance the venture for only a certain period before the business must generate enough money to be self-supporting. As a result, new business owners want to stretch their reserves as long as possible, until they reach the self-supporting stage. From this perspective, it makes good sense to spend as little money as required, and nothing on things that aren't needed.

A friend of mine, a home-business management consultant, told me a story about one of his clients, who had just begun a cleaning business. The client wanted to purchase a new computer system to keep track of clients and billing. My friend's advice to him was that he needed to go out and get more clients, and that, at that point in setting up a business, he should be spending his money on cleaning tools that would help him to get the job done better. The client's enthusiasm for expensive office equipment was a classic "cart-before-the-horse" scenario.

Unless you have an unlimited supply of money, many of the decisions that you make will be trade-offs. Features and benefits cost money. For instance, it may be convenient to install two dedicated business phone lines in addition to your home line, but the monthly costs might break your budget.

Similarly, it might be nice to provide a separate entrance for your new home office, but that might require a building application process, design services, and costly construction renovations that can be put to better use elsewhere. It is prudent to investigate less expensive solutions beforehand.

I would never advise start-up home business clients to make a burdensome initial investment in their home office environment. But I would encourage them to make all necessary investments in their personal health, their productivity, and relationships with their own clients.

How Does Home Office Design Affect My Business, My Health?

There are two groups of people in particular who must responsibly examine and respond to their home office needs, even if expenditures are required.

The first group includes any home-based business that expects to host clients. It is my firm belief that if you don't communicate an organized and professional image to your existing or potential customers, your business will survive only as long as your capital holds out. Therefore, initial decisions about office organization are critical to survival and should be thought of in that way.

The second group includes anyone who will spend substantial portions of time performing sedentary functions. This group includes corporate telecommuters, consultants, writers, lawyers, telemarketers, and in fact anyone who works primarily at a computer station, or a "desk." This has to do with productivity and health. If you are unorganized, you will not be productive. If you are uncomfortable, this will affect not only productivity, but in the long term, your personal health.

Cost Effective Solutions

A professionally organized home office doesn't necessarily require professional designers or an elaborate construction program, nor does it have to be enormously expensive.

Many solutions and products presented in this book, although relatively modest in cost, will still solve problems of organization, user comfort, and safety.

Visitors to the Home Office

If you expect to have employees or clients in your home office, the consideration of entry becomes extremely important, and the location of your office may be predetermined by entry issues.

It is always best to have a dedicated, private area for an office, if you have the luxury to choose one. However, there may be other issues that will make a less private location more suitable. For instance, that spare bedroom may be private and spacious, but if your clients visit you, and image is important, it may not be appropriate to bring them through your house to get to the office. You may be better off turning the bedroom into a den, and using the family room on the ground floor for your new office, where clients can enter more directly.

Likely Spaces for Locating a Home Office

Some of the most common spaces chosen for a home office are spare bedrooms, attics, garages, basements, and family rooms. Each choice has its drawbacks and benefits, as shown in Figure 2-1 and discussed below.

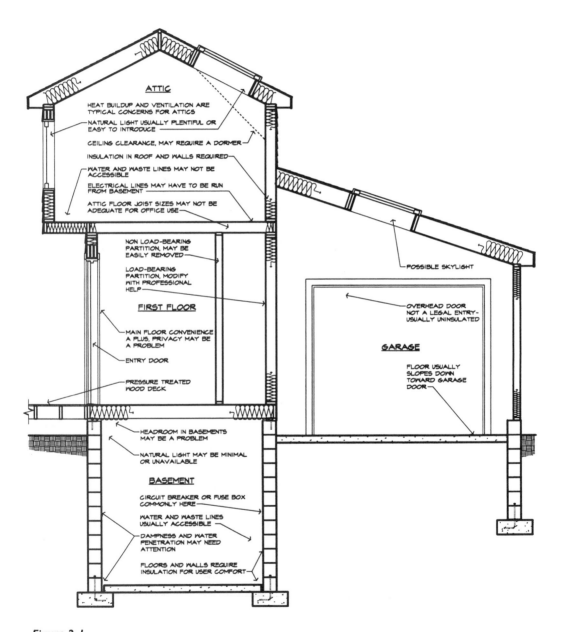

ATTIC

HEAT BUILDUP AND VENTILATION ARE TYPICAL CONCERNS FOR ATTICS

NATURAL LIGHT USUALLY PLENTIFUL OR EASY TO INTRODUCE

CEILING CLEARANCE, MAY REQUIRE A DORMER

INSULATION IN ROOF AND WALLS REQUIRED

WATER AND WASTE LINES MAY NOT BE ACCESSIBLE

ELECTRICAL LINES MAY HAVE TO BE RUN FROM BASEMENT

ATTIC FLOOR JOIST SIZES MAY NOT BE ADEQUATE FOR OFFICE USE

POSSIBLE SKYLIGHT

NON LOAD-BEARING PARTITION, MAY BE EASILY REMOVED

LOAD-BEARING PARTITION, MODIFY WITH PROFESSIONAL HELP

OVERHEAD DOOR NOT A LEGAL ENTRY- USUALLY UNINSULATED

FIRST FLOOR

MAIN FLOOR CONVENIENCE A PLUS, PRIVACY MAY BE A PROBLEM

ENTRY DOOR

GARAGE

FLOOR USUALLY SLOPES DOWN TOWARD GARAGE DOOR

PRESSURE TREATED WOOD DECK

HEADROOM IN BASEMENTS MAY BE A PROBLEM

NATURAL LIGHT MAY BE MINIMAL OR UNAVAILABLE

BASEMENT

CIRCUIT BREAKER OR FUSE BOX COMMONLY HERE

WATER AND WASTE LINES USUALLY ACCESSIBLE

DAMPNESS AND WATER PENETRATION MAY NEED ATTENTION

FLOORS AND WALLS REQUIRE INSULATION FOR USER COMFORT

Figure 2-1
Choosing a home office location; opportunities and problems associated with various spaces in a single-family home.

Adaptive Architecture, Albany, NY.

Spare Bedroom Dedicated to Home Office

This is an easy choice, because a spare bedroom is already prepared in many most ways to accept a home office. The space is usually regular in shape, has natural light, ventilation, heat, and perhaps air conditioning, and some electrical power. The walls, floors and ceilings are typically finished, as opposed to an unfinished attic or garage, and there is usually a clothes closet that can easily be converted into an office storage closet. A bedroom can be closed off, thereby offering privacy. Even a smaller bedroom is usually at least 80 square feet, which is enough space for a modest office for one person who works mainly with letter size documents. Larger bedrooms can accommodate two people.

Bedroom space may present problems if you have an employee or a client, especially if the bedroom is amid others, and is not directly accessible to the entry. If you are in a situation where you need to hire someone, marching him or her into the recesses of your home may be enough of a turnoff for a potential employee to reject an offer, even if the job is appealing. Clients certainly need more separation.

Bedroom and Office Combined

Another commonly chosen location for home offices is in the master bedroom. This is usually a quiet and separated place in the house, and it is usually one of the larger rooms. There is usually space to accommodate a desk, which may have been there even before the home office was contemplated. The space is finished, has light and air, and some electrical power. A bathroom is usually nearby. So in many ways, it becomes a natural for the home office.

The problem with setup in a bedroom is that it usually has many distractions, such as a television and a bed. People report that they find it hard to separate work and home activities when their office is in their bedroom. Another problem is that your mate may want or need to go to sleep at a time when you need to continue working.

An unmade bed can make it hard for some people to stay in a focused, business-like mood. The other side of the coin is that part of this intimate living space is now being given over to some very unromantic items, such as copying machines.

Certainly if you are living alone, it makes the situation a little less strained. If your bedroom is large enough so that you can screen off your office area, it will effect a major improvement.

If you are working in a bedroom, you will most likely need an extremely efficient and versatile workstation area. This may be a time and place to consider a manufactured "office-in-a-cabinet," because when you close it up, it looks more like an armoire than it does a workstation.

All the issues of employee or client access that were considered in discussing use of a spare bedroom apply as much—perhaps more—to the use of the master bedroom.

Attic Space   An attic usually has the advantage of being spare space, except for some storage, and of being remote from other functions of the house. There are also some romantic aspects of the "garret" quality that an attic may provide. Throw in a skylight and you're communing with the heavens. Attic spaces are usually dryer than basements, and may be warmer if insulated properly.

The basic considerations in using attic space are insulation, heat and air conditioning, and power requirements. In warmer climates, or during the warmer weather in winter climates, unconditioned attic temperatures can rise to above 140 degrees; even with heavy roof insulation, the temperature in an attic can be unbearable. You will most likely have to consider some level of air conditioning if you intend to work in an attic space.

As with spare bedrooms, it is important to consider how clients and/or employees will enter.

Garage Space   A garage offers interesting potential for a home office. It might already have a separate exterior door entrance, which could be turned into an office entrance. The floor level of a garage is usually at or close to the main level of the house, and may even be connected to it. The garage may have some electrical power available.

Garage floors are typically uninsulated concrete slabs; also, they are usually at least four to six inches below living space, to comply with building codes. An uninsulated concrete slab is extremely cold during the winter months. Even if you raise the ambient temperature to 75 degrees, the temperature at the floor could remain at 55 degrees. If you tend to sit in one place for most of the day, your body heat will be radiated into the slab, and you will tend to feel cold, especially in your legs and feet. This could be remedied by introducing insulating material over the slab.

The slope of the floor may also be an annoyance. You can solve the insulation and leveling problems at the same time, by constructing a level wood frame over the existing slab, and insulating the cavities below a new wood deck surface.

You will most likely want to insulate the walls and roof of the garage and consider a heating system, which may simply bridge off your existing system, or may be independent. An overhead garage door is usually uninsulated, and has many air spaces around the perimeter, where it meets the cased opening of the garage. Furthermore, a garage door is not considered a legal means of egress. If you plan on using your garage for an office, and especially if you plan on having any employees or visitors, you will have to check with your town for their regulations on use of a garage for a home office.

If you have a two-car garage, you might consider separating one bay for an office, and maintaining the other for a car and/or general storage needs. You probably have considerable storage, home repair tools, lawn equipment, and the like. One solution is to assemble a prefabricated metal building at another location on the building lot, within which you may store displaced equipment.

One of the nice features about converting a garage to office use is that many garages have gable roof areas that can be open to the room, adding a soaring feeling to the space. Also, with the addition of a skylight, the garage could be very light, airy and open.

Family Room, Living Room, or Den

Family rooms and dens can make great home offices, because they are often on ground level, they are one of the larger rooms in the house, and they may have architectural features, such as a brick-hearth fireplace, or a cathedral ceiling, or sliding doors to an open deck at the rear yard.

The family room is often accessible to an entry door, which comes in handy if you expect visitors. They won't have to traipse through your entire living quarters before arriving within the confines of your office. Family room space is usually finished, so there may be renovation savings in the use of this space.

A possible drawback to working in a family room is that it is often open to spaces such as stairways or kitchens, which tend to receive a lot of family traffic and noise. This problem can be partially controlled by portable, removable screens.

You may still wish to use this room as a family room, when you aren't working in it. It may be possible to arrange the family room to serve double duty, by screening off an area for office use (if the room is large enough), or by purchasing a self-contained office furniture system. Some of these look like wall units when closed, and will blend in nicely with a family room environment.

An Office in the Kitchen

Many successful businesses have been started right on the kitchen table, although I feel that this is probably the poorest candidate for a home office, and should be considered only as a temporary measure.

If the kitchen table is your location of last and only resort, then you will have to pack your office and store it somewhere else, probably every evening before dinner. You are going to have to consider what it is that you absolutely need, and departmentalize some work activities in other locations. For instance, you may have to keep your file cabinet in another location, and bring out only one file at a time, for use at the kitchen. Alternatively, you may get a rolling file cabinet, which can be moved into a remote location at supper time. Perhaps your computer is a "notebook" style, and printouts get done in another location in the house.

I caution you that this kind of compartmentalization, although possible, results in functional inefficiencies and can lead to frustration. It is hard to make the best use of your time when you have to go into another room each time you need to review a file, or get a paper clip.

Basement Space

Basement spaces usually offer privacy and quiet. Some basements open out to grade, and are called walk-out basements. These arrangements are especially nice for home offices, because they extend directly to the outdoors, and the door or sliding doors often bring in natural light to the basement area.

Basements usually have large areas of open space from which all the functions of a one-person, or even two-person office can be organized. Electrical panels and heating systems are located in the basement, making it relatively easy to branch off for heat and power. The telephone terminal blocks are usually located in the basement.

Basement floors, however, are often uninsulated concrete slabs, which can be very cold in the winter. Sometimes the ceilings, or other obstructions such as pipes or ducts, create headroom problems. If the basement is "unfinished," you may want to consider finishing the walls and floor, to keep warm in the winter if for nothing else.

Another potential drawback to using basement space might be the issue of visitors or employees. Bringing employees or clients through a living environment in order to get to the office may create negatives. If visitors are not an issue, then a basement is a plausible place to set up shop.

Most basements have small, high windows that do not afford much natural light or views.

Basements are often very damp, which can be controlled by the use of a dehumidifier. It is important to keep your machinery and your papers protected and dry. Sometimes basements have water leaks, or are prone to flooding. Be certain that these problems are corrected before setting up an office in a space that may take on water.

Working in a Hallway Area

I have seen this as a solution, and it is intriguing (see Chapter 14, Finishing with Style). If you don't have employees or young children, this arrangement can work. If family members pass your office as they go from one location to another, you will have to respect their right to breach your office territory with unexpected regularity; they will have to respect your need for quiet when they pass through, or when they are in nearby rooms. With a bit of cooperation, and in the right family mix, this can work.

The nice part of this arrangement is that you don't get in the way of other living spaces, and other than the traffic problem, this area is private to you. Depending upon the shape, length and size of the hall area, you can create a linear, or galley arrangement, and perhaps close or fold away some of your surfaces or equipment when not in use. Ideally the hall will have a large window, or some natural light, perhaps from a skylight, or borrowed from an adjacent space.

**Office in a
Walk-In Closet**

I have seen this done successfully. After all, most paneled workstation systems in traditional office space are nothing more than closets without doors and ceilings. An office in a house closet is clearly one-person space that doesn't receive visitors.

In order to turn a walk-in closet into reasonable work space you will have to introduce features that offset that "closed-in" feeling.

Hopefully, the door will be within eyeshot of a large window, so you will at least receive "borrowed" light in the closeted area. You may even wish to take the door off the hinges, and perhaps widen the remaining door opening. You might be able to cut a pass-through opening in one of the closet walls, into which you can introduce louver doors, which you can open for light and air.

Light colors, strip lighting, and shallow profiles will make the closeted space seem larger, and ultimately, make it more comfortable for you.

Your machinery, lighting, and your own body will generate heat that won't be dissipated in a small closet. You therefore will need a strategically placed fan somewhere in the closet, which will force the air to be exchanged with air outside the closet. Also, you must keep the door open while you are working.

**Office in a Wide,
Shallow Closet**

Closets with louver doors or sliding doors may be excellent candidates for internal reconfiguration into a home office. Long work surfaces supported by file cabinets can be placed or built into the closet; the upper wall can be used for storage shelves. It is likely that the doors will have to be removed during construction, or changed.

The beauty of this arrangement is that the office "disappears" when the doors are closed. Issues of privacy, clients, and employees are to be addressed as in any other location. What to do with the stuff you had in the closet is yet another consideration.

**Locations
and Floor
Finishes**

Floor finishes are important in the planning of home office space. Once you choose a location, you may need to consider changing the floor surface, for the following reasons.

Floors in offices are subject to more intense wear than floors in homes, not only because of foot traffic, but also because of the constant movement and rolling around of chairs and other equipment.

If you choose carpet for your office, you will want to be sure that it is of the low-static type; electronic equipment is very vulnerable to static shock. If you are working on existing carpet and you are receiving static shocks, speak with your local equipment suppliers about static electricity grounding methods and devices. You may also be able to treat your carpet for static retardation; a local retail carpeting outfit may be able to help you.

Loop, as opposed to cut-pile, carpet is generally a better pick for an office, because it is easier to keep clean, and you can roll a chair on it more easily.

Wood floors provide a warmth and "homeyness"; some patterned wood floors are a visual pleasure. Another nice feature about wood floors is that they offer little rolling resistance, when compared with carpet. Wood floors generate little or no static electricity.

The grain of wood floors may be stained easily, and may be damaged by continual rolling-over of chair wheels. You may wish to consider some protection in the heavy-wear areas, especially where rolling chairs are located.

Tile or linoleum floors can be very attractive, and they offer the added advantage of being easily maintained, less subject to staining. Tile floors can be designed in a variety of colors and patterns, adding visual interest to a space.

Planning a Renovation or Addition

If you are living in a condominium apartment, you may be considering an interior renovation to provide you with work space. If you own a single family residence, you may be considering a major renovation and/or addition that will be dedicated to your home office. If this is the case, please be sure to read Chapter 13, Renovations, Additions, and New Construction.

Thinking It Over

After you have carefully analyzed your basic office requirements, and compared what you need with what space you have available, you may rightfully decide that a home office just isn't practical for your situation. Sometimes there is just no practical way to blend an office for a particular kind of work with a specific lifestyle, or within a specific piece of real estate.

That said, it is my belief that in most situations, a home office can be accommodated with a little bit of planning, flexibility, cooperation, and common sense.

Last, be sure to check with local authorities before converting space in your home for use as a home office.

CHAPTER THREE
PLANNING FOR WORKSTATIONS

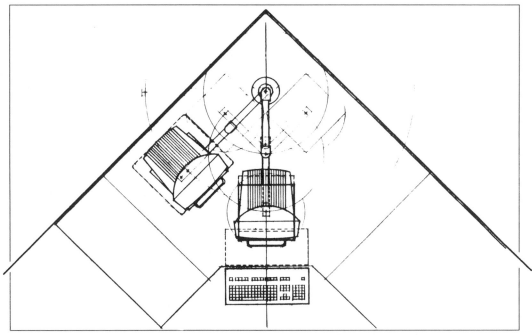

Drawing Courtesy of Roger Gohl Design Studio, Los Angeles, CA.

W ORKSTATIONS ARE AT THE HEART of the working home office. They are where you will spend most of your time. After analyzing your requirements, you will probably find that you need more than one workstation, or that your workstation will have to be multifunctional.

Importance of Organization

In your home, you are blending a work situation with a living situation, which will involve at least your own personal life, if not that of others. In this situation, it is doubly important to be organized, as a means of defining clear separation between what is "home" and what is "office." Organization is a form of discipline, and ultimately, discipline is the key to success at working independently.

Unless you have the luxury of abundant living quarters, you will probably want to make every square inch of your home office useful. A well-organized and versatile workstation will take maximum advantage of allocated space.

Workstations and Personal Wellness

Health hazards are different than they used to be. During the industrial age, people sustained terrible physical injuries which sometimes required surgery and hospitalization. Eventually, federal laws were enacted to protect workers. Now eyestrain, carpal tunnel syndrome, and back injury are the new health hazards of the so-called "information age." Although they aren't as immediate or apparent as a sudden injury in a factory, they are often equally serious. In addition to being productive, your workstation should also be healthful (see Chapter 6, Ergonomics).

Energy

Power and communication feeds will be required at most workstations in order for them to be functional.

Energy requirements for work spaces have been discussed in Chapter 1, Home Office Planning "101" and are reviewed in further detail in Chapter 4, Electrical Power Requirements. Also, power symbols are shown on the planning illustrations in Chapter 5, Puttin' It All Together.

Employees

If you plan to have an employee, it will have an effect on issues beyond workstation planning, which we've covered in previous chapters. Even if the employee is part-time, he or she will probably need a dedicated project station. If the employee is full-time, a dedicated project station will be a virtual requirement. You may be able to share other workstations with an employee, which will require scheduling on your part.

If you plan to have more than one employee, you are stepping across the threshold into "small-office," which will place more demands on your privacy issues and support spaces. More employees will also impact entry and parking issues, and your town will most likely be more restrictive. Small office design is the subject of another book, as-yet unwritten.

Determining the Number and Type of Workstations

The acronym C-A-M-P may help you to remember the four basic workstation configurations: computer, administrative, meeting, and projects. Depending on the nature of your work, you will need one or more of these workstation groups.

If you are a corporate telecommuter, you may need only one workstation, and that will probably be a computer workstation. Read about the organization of all four station types, and then you be the judge.

Regardless of your situation, you must plan for all your task requirements, or you will sink in a sea of confusion and disorganization, instead of becoming a productive home office worker.

C Computer Workstations

Just about everybody who works at home today uses a computer, even if it is just for a few hours per week. Some home workers will spend most of their working hours at their computer workstation.

Computer workstations have the greatest power requirements of any home office workstation arrangement. This is partly because of the variety of peripheral devices and partly because of communications demands.

The physical structure of the computer workstation is (and should be) different from a standard desk or work surface. I mention this because a computer workstation in itself will not be suitable to double as an administrative or meeting station. It will also be unsuitable for doubling as a project station, unless of course, the project station is a computer station.

If you use a portable computer, such as a laptop or notebook, and if your computer use is fairly light, you may not need a dedicated computer workstation. In this case your

ITEM NAME	MODEL/MFR	DIMENSIONS (LxWxH)	ELEC.	TEL.	COMMENTS
COMPUTER PROCESSOR					
VIDEO DATA TERMINAL					
KEYBOARD					
PRINTER					
MODEM					
SCANNER					
OTHER EXTERNALS					
COPY EASEL					
KEYBOARD TRAY					
MOUSE TRAY					
WRIST REST					
ARM RESTS					
PROCESSOR MOUNTER					
ADJUSTABLE MONITOR ARM					
TASK LIGHT					
TELEPHONE					
DISK STORAGE					
PROGRAM MANUALS					
PRINTER PAPER					

Figure 3-1
Computer station checklist.

administrative workstation might double as your computer workstation. Some companies are making small, roll-about workstations designed specifically for light-use notebook computer work (see Chapter 9, Workstation Furniture).

In order to help you sort out and keep track of your specific needs for a computer station, Figure 3.1 details a computer station checklist for you. Notice that the checklist has columns in which you can list specific information about equipment. Not only is this handy as a permanent record of what you have, but it will also help you to size and outfit your station. Lastly, it will help you to determine the necessary utility requirements at the workstation location.

A
Administrative
Workstations

In corporate-office parlance, "administrator" is a managerial title to which is attached a level of authority and status.

I use the word "administration" here to mean stewardship of your home-based business activities, pure and simple—it is unglamorous, time-consuming, and probably nonbillable. Opening and posting mail, invoicing clients, paying bills, making bank deposits, and handling the bookkeeping functions are all part of administering the home office. Owners of home-based businesses have to perform all these functions, or hire people to do them. One way or the other, space will be required, separate and apart from the computer workstation.

I am also including communications and duplication as part of the administrative function. The telephone, answering machine, fax machine, and copier will require space, power, and communications feeds in order to operate properly.

The administrative space should also provide for day-to-day storage requirements for shipping and mailing.

In Figure 3-2 you will find an administrative station checklist. Almost all of the items you will use daily are on this list. You may have other needs, which you can easily add to the list. Similar to the computer workstation checklist, there are columns where you can list size and utility requirements.

M
Meeting Stations

If you are going to have one, or at most two visitors at a time in your home office, you may be able to host them at your administrative station. The standard desk–credenza setup with two pull-up chairs may be the answer for you.

ITEM NAME	MFR/SIZE	ELEC.	TEL.	COMMENTS
POWER EQUIPMENT				
TASK LIGHT				
TELEPHONE				
RADIO				
CALCULATOR				
STAPLER				
PENCIL SHARPENER				
SPECIAL EQUIPMENT				
FILING/STORAGE				
ACTIVE PROJECT FILES				
BINDERS				
DIRECTORIES/BOOKS				
STOCK PAPER				
CHECKS/CHECKBOOK				
OVERNIGHT ENVELOPES				
MAGAZINE FILES				
PROJECT SUPPLIES				
SPECIAL STORAGE				
DESK TOOLS				
PENS/PENCILS				
STAPLER				
PAPER CLIPS				
TAPE DISPENSER				
MISC HAND TOOLS				
3 HOLE PUNCH				
WASTE BASKET				
SPECIAL TOOLS				
MISCELLANEOUS				

Figure 3-2
Administrative station checklist.

In fact, this arrangement could conceivably triple up as a computer station (the credenza), an administrative station (the desk), and pull-up chairs in front of the desk, for the meetings. This is a very space intensive arrangement, however, which involves superb and constant organization, in order to remain respectable to the visitors, and sane for the user. Remember, however, that entry and separation issues still prevail when it comes to meetings, as discussed in prior chapters.

If you plan to conduct group meetings, you will need a conferencing area. As discussed in previous chapters, this may be in another room in the house, perhaps a room that does double service; or it may be a remote location.

If you are going to have even one regular employee, you will not only need a workstation for that person, but you will most likely need a meeting station simply to review work.

**P
Project
Workstations**

The project station is the epicenter of the home office. These are probably the most variable workstation types, because work functions and styles are vastly variable. Graphic artists, lawyers, claims processors, sales people, accountants, all will have different project station requirements. Even within the same line of business, individual styles and requirements will vary. Understanding how you work, and what you need to do a project will be key to determining workstation size, which is the very next task.

Although project stations vary widely from one user to another, many of the tools and pieces of equipment are similar. Similar to the checklists for computer and administrative stations, a project station checklist is given in Figure 3-3.

**Combining
(Multifunction)
Workstations**

Your particular work style may allow you to combine two or more workstation types. Space limitations may force you consider "doubling up." Before you make any decisions, you should consider how much work surface you need. Sample workstation arrangements in Figures 3-4 through 3-9, later in this chapter, may give you some ideas.

**Determining
the Size of
Each Work
Surface**

After you have decided which combination of workstations you will require, you have to decide on size. The place to start is by determining how much work surface you need. Only then can you evaluate and organize the space you intend to allocate for office use (see Chapter 5, Puttin' It All Together).

ITEM NAME	MFR/SIZE	ELEC.	TEL.	COMMENTS
POWER EQUIPMENT				
TASK LIGHT				
TELEPHONE				
ANSWERING MACHINE				
RADIO				
FACSIMILE MACHINE				
COPIER				
CALCULATOR				
STAPLER				
PENCIL SHARPENER				
POSTAGE METER				
FILING/STORAGE				
BOOKKEEPG/ACCTG				
OTHER BUSINESS RECORDS				
DIRECTORIES/BOOKS				
STATIONERY				
CHECKS/CHECKBOOK				
MAILING ENVELOPES				
STAMPS				
DESK TOOLS				
PENS/PENCILS				
STAPLER				
PAPER CLIPS				
TAPE DISPENSER				
MISC HAND TOOLS				
ADDRESS BOOK/FILE				
POSTAGE SCALE				
POSTAGE METER				
WASTE BASKET				
MISCELLANEOUS				

Figure 3-3
Project station checklist.

This Is Getting Overwhelming— Where Do I Start?

Perhaps there is a workstation you use somewhere else, which you can measure for size. You may also get some assistance from a furniture dealer, or a design professional.

You can also do it on your own, from scratch. We're going to give you the tools and the steps. We've provided fairly thorough checklists of the kinds of things you will need for computer, administrative, and project stations right here in this chapter. Photocopy these checklists, and fill in the stuff you need for your stations. Be sure to check off the boxes if telephone or electric power is needed, which will come in handy later. Above all, make sure to measure the sizes of things, and put them in the dimension box.

1. Figure out how much computer station space you will need. Turn to Chapter 7, Workstation Furniture, and pick out a configuration that you think will work for you, based on the array and sizes of equipment you use. Allow three feet of width for a roll-about, four feet for a small workstation, and five feet for a larger one. If you are planning on a larger station, such as a ready-to-assemble wall unit, then get the actual size from a dealer or manufacturer.

2. Administrative station needs will be pretty much the same from one home office to another, unless you have unusual storage or shipping requirements. You should be able to do everything on a 30 × 60 inch horizontal surface that is 29 to 30 inches off the floor. You can store files and supplies in file cabinets below the surface, or on shelves on the wall. You can scale this standard up, or down, depending on your specific requirements, and the space you have available.

3. Decide if you will need a meeting station, and if so, how many people it will serve, and where it will be. Remember that if you have a part time employee, you will need a small, but appropriate (hopefully not the kitchen table!) meeting station.

4. Decide how much project station "lay-space" you will need. This is simply a designer word for how much flat surface you need to do your thing. If you are a map maker, you will need more lay space than if you are a writer. If you are a lawyer, you may need a large table to lay out a case. Also, don't forget busy seasons—an accountant may need more lay-space around tax time.

Sample Workstation Arrangements

As a conclusion to this chapter, we've provided a number of workstation layouts that may be suitable for your needs. They will ultimately have to be matched up against your existing space. Some of these arrangements are multifunctional, providing surfaces and storage areas for various combinations of workstation configurations.

Straight

This layout, shown in Figure 3-4, is a variation of the old-fashioned, "desk pushed up against a wall," except that it can be customized for width and length, and it makes excellent use of wall space above, for filing and storage. A

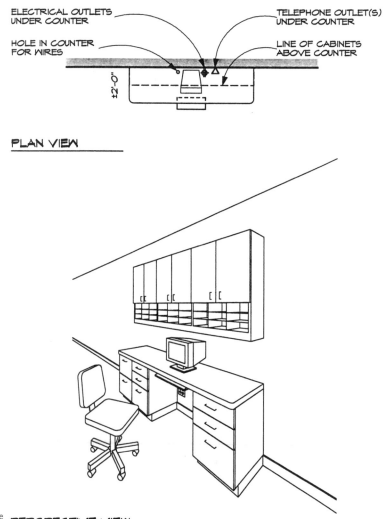

ELECTRICAL OUTLETS UNDER COUNTER

TELEPHONE OUTLET(S) UNDER COUNTER

HOLE IN COUNTER FOR WIRES

LINE OF CABINETS ABOVE COUNTER

±2'-0"

PLAN VIEW

PERSPECTIVE VIEW

Figure 3-4
Straight workstation arrangement.
Courtesy of Magnusson Architecture & Planning, P. C., New York, NY.

fluorescent strip light below the wall cabinet can evenly light the work surface.

This arrangement is good for any room, or even a narrow hallway. Take a look at the various modular and paneled workstation configurations in Chapter 7.

Corner   A corner arrangement, as shown in Figure 3-5, provides layout space on each side of a computer station. Leg room is an important consideration in the design of a corner station.

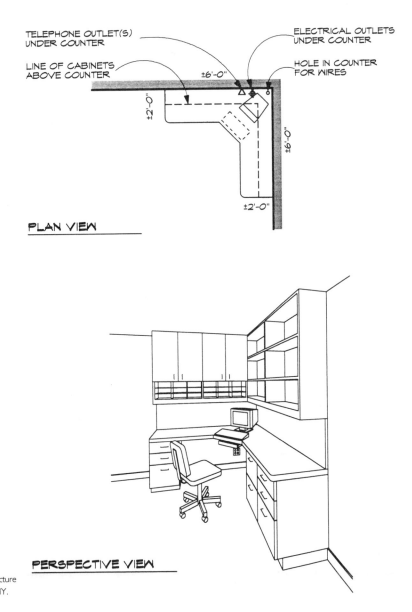

TELEPHONE OUTLET(S) UNDER COUNTER

LINE OF CABINETS ABOVE COUNTER

ELECTRICAL OUTLETS UNDER COUNTER

HOLE IN COUNTER FOR WIRES

±6'-0"

±2'-0"

±6'-0"

±2'-0"

PLAN VIEW

PERSPECTIVE VIEW

Figure 3-5
Corner workstation
arrangement.
Courtesy of Magnusson Architecture
& Planning, P. C., New York, NY.

U-Shaped   This variation on corporate workstations in a private office is shown in Figure 3-6. It is a combination of computer, project/administrative, and meeting stations, all rolled into one. Again, excellent use is made of wall filing and storage.

Galley   This double-loaded arrangement, shown in Figure 3-7, is composed of two "straights." It is suitable in a long narrow room, or even in a wide hallway. If wide enough, two people may work independently on either side.

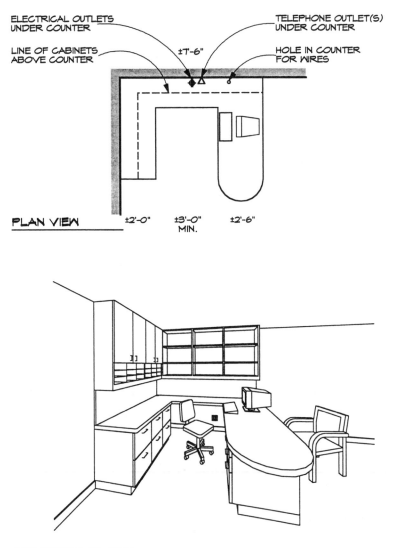

Figure 3-6
U-shaped workstation
arrangement.
Courtesy of Magnusson Architecture
& Planning, P. C., New York, NY.

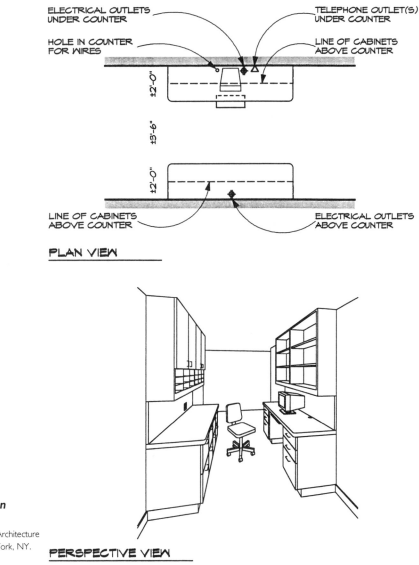

ELECTRICAL OUTLETS
UNDER COUNTER

TELEPHONE OUTLET(S)
UNDER COUNTER

HOLE IN COUNTER
FOR WIRES

LINE OF CABINETS
ABOVE COUNTER

±2'-0"

±3'-6"

±2'-0"

LINE OF CABINETS
ABOVE COUNTER

ELECTRICAL OUTLETS
ABOVE COUNTER

PLAN VIEW

PERSPECTIVE VIEW

Figure 3-7
Galley workstation
arrangement.
Courtesy of Magnusson Architecture
& Planning, P. C., New York, NY.

Alcove   A variation on the U shape, an alcove arrangement, such as that shown in Figure 3-8, is suitable for a nook in an apartment; it can also be configured in a large, walk-in closet if one wall can be opened for light. If large enough, it may be developed into three independent workstation zones.

Closet   A shallow but wide closet can be nicely converted into a station, as shown in Figure 3-9. It has the added feature of being able to screen the work zone when not in use by closing the doors. This is especially nice for an office in a bedroom, a family room, or in a small apartment.

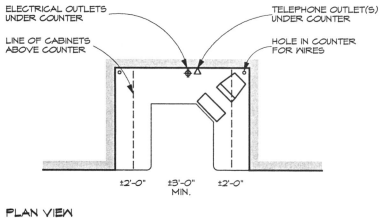

ELECTRICAL OUTLETS
UNDER COUNTER

TELEPHONE OUTLET(S)
UNDER COUNTER

LINE OF CABINETS
ABOVE COUNTER

HOLE IN COUNTER
FOR WIRES

±2'-0"   ±3'-0"   ±2'-0"
                 MIN.

PLAN VIEW

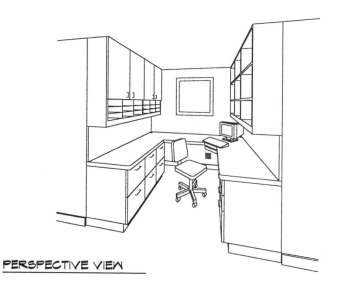

Figure 3-8
Alcove workstation
arrangement.
Courtesy of Magnusson Architecture
& Planning, P. C., New York, NY.

PERSPECTIVE VIEW

Other Ideas   You can get more ideas from the Chapter 7, Workstation
Furniture, where you will find a broad range of configurations and workstation combinations.

You can make up your own layout on a piece of graph
paper. If each box represents ½ inch, you will probably be
able to get one station on an $8\frac{1}{2} \times 11$ inch page. If each box
represents ¼ inch, you may be able to get a whole room
onto a page, which is where we're headed. We'll "put it all
together" when we get to Chapter 5.

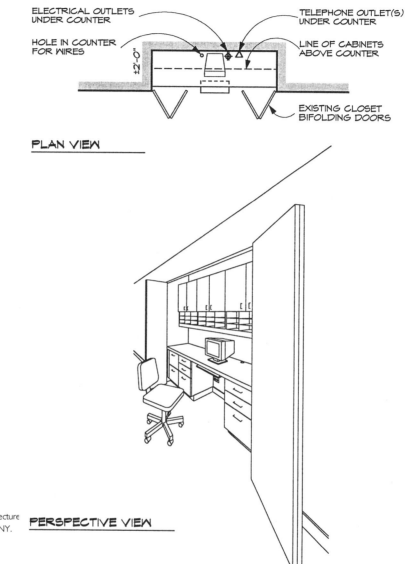

ELECTRICAL OUTLETS
UNDER COUNTER

TELEPHONE OUTLET(S)
UNDER COUNTER

HOLE IN COUNTER
FOR WIRES

LINE OF CABINETS
ABOVE COUNTER

±2'-0"

EXISTING CLOSET
BIFOLDING DOORS

PLAN VIEW

Figure 3-9
Closet workstation
arrangement.
Courtesy of Magnusson Architecture
& Planning, P. C., New York, NY.

PERSPECTIVE VIEW

CHAPTER FOUR
ELECTRICAL POWER REQUIREMENTS

Configuration from the TD Collection.
Courtesy of Herman Miller for the Home, Zeeland, MI. Photo by Elliot Kaufman Photography.

R ELIABLE AND ADEQUATE ELECTRICAL POWER for equipment and communications is critical to the successful operation of any office. Because it is relatively "invisible" compared with equipment, furniture and decor, we often tend to give it less than the priority it deserves. The power required to run a home office, even a small one, may be different and more intense than what is normally provided in residential spaces such as bedrooms and family rooms.

It is an almost universal fact that we never seem to have enough power outlets. When you inventory the power requirements of all your equipment, which may be operating all at once, including lights, perhaps a window air conditioner, or that little space heater you use in the winter, you may require not only more outlets, but one or more additional circuits.

Trial and Error

If you choose to experiment—by setting up, plugging in, and seeing what happens—you may experience power failures, equipment damage, or your devices may be strained, which will affect their longevity and even daily operation. You may degrade the power supply units in some electronic equipment, and you may also cause your computer to "crash."

Analyzing Power Needs

Similar to surveying your work space requirements, you should survey the power requirements for all of your plug-in devices.

You may start by making a list of all your desktop equipment, using the sample list provided in Figure 4-1.

The list offers typical requirements for generic equipment, but it's important for you to get the power requirements for your specific devices. You can find out the amperage draws for each device from the manuals, or on rating labels at the back of your machines. The ratings are usually given in amps, with the voltage often given. Units that are also sold in the European market may have dual voltage capabilities. If watts are given, you can divide by 11 to get the current in amps.

Power Circuits and Overload

A circuit is a continuous loop of power, upon which several outlets are typically attached. If too much equipment is plugged into one circuit, it will shut down. To avoid this, you have to know which outlets are on which circuits. You can do this by trial and error—that is, by going to the power (circuit breaker) box, and shutting off circuits one at a time, to see which outlets are affected.

To determine the load (amount of total power demand) on a given circuit, simply total the amps for each piece of equipment you plan to plug into it. Most circuits are designed for a load of 15 amps. It is recommended that you have no more than 12 amps on a 15 amp circuit, and 16 amps on a 20 amp circuit.

For a small office with two computers, a printer, telephone, and fax, a single circuit should suffice. If an air conditioner or heater is used, it should be on a separate circuit. The list in Figure 4-1 provides typical amperage for some equipment. You can use this chart to complete your list, but be sure to check power requirements for each piece of your own equipment, because it may vary from typical values shown.

Surplus Outlets

During the course of time, you may wish to move equipment from one location to another or add simple items like electric pencil sharpeners, another lamp, or an additional piece of peripheral computer equipment that needs power. If you decide to add outlets, consider adding a few extra ones, spread evenly throughout your space. They will come in handy at a future date, especially when you are using tools like a vacuum.

Utility Service and Protection

The quality of power delivery from utility companies varies from one location to another. If your neighborhood has frequent power outages, "brownouts," or power fluctuations, you may want to consider purchasing an uninterrupted power supply (UPS) with a line conditioner. These devices provide security in two ways: First, in the event of an outage, they will give you enough power to save data and safely shut down equipment. Second, and perhaps equally important, they will assure a moderated, "clean" power supply to your machine, which may improve performance, reduce repair costs, and increase longevity of the system.

There are two major types of UPS units available: back-up, and line-conditioning. Both units provide power during brownouts or power outages, and usually contain surge suppression as well as noise filtering. The back-up type is

Equipment	Current (amps)	Surge Suppressor	UPS	Comments
Computer with 300 watt supply	2.7	Yes	Yes	
Monitor 14" to 15"	1.5	Yes	Yes	
Monitor 17"	1.9	Yes	Yes	
Monitor 20"	2.4	Yes	Yes	
External Modem	0.1	Yes	Yes	
External Disk & CD ROM Drives	0.2	Yes	Yes	
Peripherals large	check	Yes	Yes	A
Peripherals small	0.1	Yes	Yes	
Printer, large Laser, HP4SIMX	9.4	Yes	No	B
Printer medium Laser, HPIII	7.6	Yes	No	
Printer personal Laser, HPIIIP	6.0	Yes	No	B
Printer Ink jet	0.4	Yes	No	
Printer Dot matrix	1.0	Yes	No	
Plotter, Ink jet E size , HP Design Jet 650	2.0	Yes	No	
Plotter, Pen E size, HP Draftmaster	1.5	Yes	No	
Self power speakers	0.1	Yes	No	
Telephone	0.1	Yes	No	
Telephone line (s)	NA	Yes	NA	
Answering machine	0.1	Yes	No	
Fax machine	1.5	Yes	No	
Copy Machine Medium	13.0	No	No	B, D
Desk light	0.5	No	No	
Heater Portable	12.5	No	No	C, D
Coffee maker	7.5	No	No	D
Small refrigerator	1.5	No	No	D
Large refrigerator (house hold)	6.5	No	No	D
Room lighting	1 to 2	No	No	
Room Air conditioning	check	No	No	D
Room Electric Heat	check	No	No	D

A) Only put essential equipment on the UPS required for a graceful shut down of your system.

B) Laser printers and copy machines require the most power, due to motors that handle the paper and heaters that melt the toner.

C) The use of a portable electric heater is not recommended. Their power requirements are high. Room heating should be on a separate circuit and provided by a fixed unit.

D) Units that contain motors or cycle on and off should be on separate circuit from your electronic office equipment. These units cause voltage surges (spikes) and sags on the power lines and can cause damage and equipment malfunction on sensitive electronic equipment.

Figure 4-1

Typical office equipment power requirements.

Courtesy of Kuegler Associates, Consulting Engineers, Tewksbury, MA and Oakville, CT.

the simpler and less expensive of the two. Line conditioning units provide the added benefit of regulating the voltage around a predetermined ideal, operating continuously. These units cost slightly more but provide a higher level of protection.

UPS units come in various sizes and must be chosen based on demand requirements. An undersized unit is worse than no unit at all. Laser and copy machines shouldn't be connected to these units, since the power consumed by them is much more than the typical UPS can handle. See Figure 4-1 for a list of recommendations about which equipment should be protected by UPS.

At the very least, you should invest in a surge protector, which is commonly sold as part of a multiple-outlet power strip, and is inexpensive. The surge protector senses a power surge, and cuts power before it gets into your equipment. This is a small investment that yields big protection. You should introduce surge protection for each piece of sensitive equipment.

It is also important to invest in a good quality surge protector. Don't be fooled by a plug-strip that has a built-in circuit breaker, one of those little red buttons on the side, which are unnecessary. There are many different types of surge suppressors on the market, and some are better than others at protecting your equipment.

Even the best surge supressor may fail to do its job during severe lightning storms. It is a good idea to unplug the entire system from power and phone lines during a storm, if possible. Remember that lightning can travel through a phone line into your modem, destroying it and the computer connected to it. Another safety measure is to check with the telephone company to see that all ground connections are tight, and that a "network interface" is in place. See Figure 4-1 for a list of recommended equipment for protection by a surge protector.

Grounding

It is very important for all equipment to be grounded, which will occur if the three-pin power plug is inserted into a three-pin female outlet that is also grounded. Do not assume that because the outlet has three pins and directly accepts the plug, that it is properly grounded. You can purchase a testing device with which you can verify grounding, or you can have an electrician test it for you.

Static and Equipment Sensitivity

Static is an enemy of sensitive electronic equipment. A carpeted room can help you to develop a static charge on yourself that can be discharged through your keyboard, easily blowing out the motherboard on your computer. If you are choosing carpet, you should select a product that is designed for reduced static, and that is appropriate for use with electronic components.

Heat Generation and Climate Control

Everything that uses power generates heat. Additional heat created by several devices running simultaneously could raise room temperature beyond the comfort level. If you choose a location in your home that is ordinarily difficult to keep cool, you can be certain that the introduction of office equipment will only increase the problem.

You may have the opportunity in your home office to ventilate your home naturally, by opening windows, doors, or operable skylights. Nevertheless, when you have all your equipment running, the lights are on, and it's Phoenix in July, you will most likely require additional cooling.

The direction your office faces, the number and size of windows, building insulation, trees and other shading devices, and your latitude location will all affect the comfort level of your space, which will vary at different times of the year, and under differing weather conditions.

If you choose to install an air conditioning unit, this will be an additional load on the power consumption within your home office.

Heat and Machinery Sensitivity

Electronic equipment is designed to operate within a range of temperatures that match human comfort levels. Machinery is sensitive to extreme temperatures, especially heat, and also to humidity. Paper doesn't move through printers and copiers well in very humid environments. High ambient temperatures can do permanent damage to equipment components.

Communications

At present, it is common for home offices to communicate with the outside world using one or more of these media: telephone (voice), modem (computer), and facsimile (text). Connection between points for all three modes is made via one or more telephone lines.

Although it's possible to use one telephone line for all three modes, in most cases it is not practical to do so. It is very difficult to keep switching between modes during the course of a normal day of business operation. An additional phone line will be a great help and should be considered as part of the initial planning for the office.

Home office business management consultants recommend that you get a phone line separate from your residential line for business use. This is especially important if you have children. This line should be equipped with call-waiting, to prevent callers from getting a busy signal when you are on the business line.

If you use a facsimile machine and/or a computer modem regularly, it is probably a good idea to get an additional line for these two functions. You can also use this line for outgoing calls; incoming calls can then be fielded on your first line, by your answering machine, allowing you to continue your conversation uninterrupted. In order to make this method work conveniently, you should purchase a two-line phone, which will allow you voice access to either line from one telephone instrument.

Desktop video communication is yet another medium that will require connections with electrical power, communications lines, and your computer (see Chapter 12). Within less than a few years, this technology may be as common as the car telephone, and it would be wise to consider planning for it now.

Planning Summary for Electronic Equipment

The basic array of equipment in a modern home office are the computer, copier, printer, fax machine, and telephone.

The problem in planning for this equipment is that configurations and capabilities are ever changing. For instance, why plan for separate spaces for a printer, fax, and copier, when you can now have one machine that does it all?

On the other hand, if your work requires a stand-alone color copy machine that's about the size of a Volkswagen, then your requirements will be entirely different.

I've decided not to attempt to review features of individual pieces of electronic equipment in detail, as I have for workstations. If I did, by the time this book was in print, everything would be obsolete anyway.

I thought it would be best to talk about technology from a conceptual planning point of view. The important points to consider, when you are planning your office to accommodate electronic equipment, are the following:

1. *Plan for everything.* Make a thorough list of all pieces of equipment that you are planning to use. There are the five basics above, and anything else you use in your business, such as scanners, other external peripherals, graphics, camera equipment, and the like (see Figure 4-1).

2. *Measure everything.* On separate paper, draw squares or rectangles that represent the "footprint" of the equipment. Also measure height, and consider if paper is going in or out of the sides of the equipment.

3. *Think about space **around** your equipment.* For example, copying machines have paper feed trays that are normally on the side of the machine. Not only do they themselves take up space, but you may need even more room on the side to remove them. Consider that you may need a surface or bin to catch the paper that rolls out of your fax machine. Remember also that almost all equipment produces heat that is ventilated from the sides and top. If you jam equipment into tight spots or otherwise prevent air circulation, you can damage your equipment.

4. *Consider the height of your equipment.* For example, a copier may be inconvenient to use if you put it on a high counter, or your computer may not fit into the roll-top desk you would like to purchase.

5. *Consider room for peripherals.* Photographs often show computers sitting comfortably on a small desk, but if you have externals that attach to your computer, you may not have enough surface area to comfortably provide for everything.

6. *List the electrical requirements of each piece of equipment.* This may take a little work—you may have to check the operating manuals, or call the manufacturer. It is rare that a piece of equipment needs a dedicated circuit these days, but an accumulation of too many pieces of equipment on the same line can result in data loss, equipment damage over time, or intermittent power outages. By tallying power, you can determine whether you have enough circuits, how many outlets you will need, and how the equipment should be distributed among the outlets. You may also be tipped off about the need for

surge protectors, which are inexpensive today, and should be provided for every piece of sensitive electronic equipment.

7. *Consider heat.* Almost all equipment generates some heat, even in an idling mode. Added up, piece by piece, including lighting, the heat can become substantial, affecting your own comfort, and jeopardizing the safety of the equipment and data. Power consumption and heat generation are important preliminary considerations when planning for an office and selecting an appropriate location.

8. *Expect change, even if you can't exactly plan for it.* It's hard to keep up with the rapid change in electronic technology. Manufacturers tell me that in some cases, a new design concept becomes obsolete even before it goes into production. With the arrival of multifunction devices, you may eventually wind up with an extra piece of space, which of course will be filled by some as yet uninvented piece of new equipment. That's life in the information fast lane.

Creating a Graphic Plan for Power Requirements

As you can see, electrical and communications planning can get complicated. The best way to get control over this is to make a sketch overlay, directly on a copy of a floor plan for your office (see sample hand-sketched plans in Chapter 5, Puttin' It All Together).

You can create your own symbols for duplex outlets, telephone outlets, and so on, or you can use conventional symbols. The standard symbol for a telephone outlet is a small triangle, and the standard symbol for a duplex outlet is a tiny circle with two parallel lines crossing over it. You may wish to use two colors—one for existing outlets and one for new outlets.

By going through this exercise, you will not only learn how many outlets you need, but you will be able to compare requirements with what you already have in place. Also, you will be able to indicate specific locations, and even dimension them, so that an electrician will know where to install your new outlets. The closer you are able to position an outlet to a piece of equipment, or vice versa, the less likely it is that you will need extension cords, which only increase clutter, collect dust, and are potential fire hazards.

If you are connecting more than one device to a single telephone outlet, such as a fax machine, or a modem, two-way and three-way adapters are commonly available at stores that sell electronics parts. If these various devices are separated in the office, it might be worthwhile to consider installing separate outlets for each.

If you are planning to use a two-line system, you may wish to install wiring and telephone connectors (jacks) that provide for two lines. From these outlets, a single cable will bring two separate lines to a two-line telephone instrument.

Safety First   If there is any doubt in your mind about the ability of your work space to carry the power load you will demand from it, consult with an electrical engineer or a licensed electrical contractor. Overloading of electrical circuits can be hazardous to your equipment and can also cause a fire.

If you determine that you need additional outlets, a professional can help you to plan for your requirements and provide you with an estimate for any additional outlets or circuits that may be required.

CHAPTER FIVE
PUTTIN' IT ALL TOGETHER

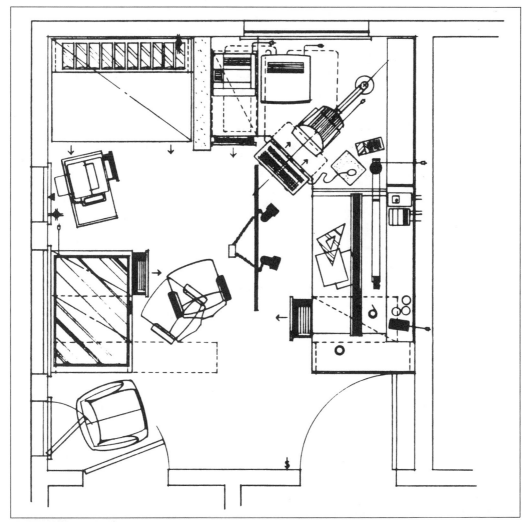

Drawing courtesy of Roger Gohl Design Studio, Los Angeles, CA

ONCE YOU HAVE CHOSEN A WORK SPACE LOCATION, and you have an idea about your workstation configuration(s), you are ready to create a simple working "floor plan" for your new home office, which merges the room features, furniture, and existing workstations together.

For the Stone-Cold Layperson: Seven Simple Steps

This method for creating a working plan assumes that you have absolutely no drafting or drawing skills. This may all be new to you, but if you want to do the job right, you should come up with a basic layout of your new home office. It will allow you to see if your ideas are feasible, and to communicate them quickly to other people who can help you, such as the phone line installer, the furniture dealer, your husband, wife, significant other, and so on.

Remember that your drawings don't have to be beautiful. You are not being graded, and you are not entering a contest.

The only thing the drawings need to do is help you test and communicate ideas.

Tools

The basic tools you will need to do this are:

- A retractable measuring tape.
- $8\frac{1}{2} \times 11$ inch sheets of graph paper (preferably four boxes to the inch). Graph paper will help you to keep your lines straight, and help you set up a standard scale.
- 12 inch ruler.
- Pencil and eraser.
- Scissors
- Mending tape and glue.

Your first task is to get a perimeter outline of the room you plan to use. A rectangular room, which is most likely what you will be working with, will be easy to draw.

Graph Paper and Cutout Method

1. Get the overall width and length of the room first, in feet and inches, and transfer your measurements to graph paper, using a single thick line to represent the perimeter wall. Work in pencil so you can easily erase. If you let $\frac{1}{2}$ inch on your paper correspond to 1 foot of actual room length, you will probably find that you can get your whole room onto one sheet of paper. Using this scale, an $8\frac{1}{2} \times 11$ inch sheet of paper will allow you to draw a room as large as 17×22 feet. If either of your dimensions

are larger, you can use a larger piece of paper (you can tape two pieces together), or you can use a smaller scale (try letting ¼ inch on the paper correspond to 1 foot of room length).

2. Measure your doors and windows, and mark them accurately onto the plan, using the same scaling system. If you measure the distance of each item from one corner of the room, you will be able to locate it in its proper location on the drawing.

3. Do the same with any radiators, columns, air vents, or anything else that might affect placement of furniture or equipment.

4. On the same drawing, make small symbols that correspond to existing telephone and electrical outlets in the room. You can use a "T" or an "E," or whatever symbol you wish, so long as you use set up a convention. Try to place the symbols as accurately as possible. You may also find it helpful to use a different color pen.

5. Measure any existing furniture pieces that you plan to have in the room, and draw them onto a separate piece of graph paper.

6. In Chapter 3, Planning for Workstations, we provided a sample number of workstation configurations. You may have developed one or more of your own. On a separate piece of graph paper, draw your workstation configurations.

7. Neatly cut out all your furniture and workstation drawings, and place them on the plan of the room, like a jigsaw puzzle, to see how everything fits. You will be able to move your cutouts around to get the optimum layout, to check clearances at doors, to see how much open space you have, to determine proximity to windows, to see if electrical oulets are where you need them, and so on.

    Note: Be sure that the scale you use to draw the room, and the scale you use to draw your furniture and workstations are the same—or else you will get incorrect results.

By using this scale and cutout system, you will be able to experiment with a number of arrangements until you get the optimum setup. When you do, you can tape or glue the cutouts to your room plan, or you can transfer the image, by carefully drawing an outline around each piece of furniture, right onto the floor plan.

for Someone with Drafting Experience

If you have drafting skills, you can simply create a "background" floor plan drawing of the room location, and make several photocopies. Working from a dimensioned inventory of furniture and workstations, you can then sketch in the items, in scale, onto a copy of the background. By using copies, you can keep tossing them away until you get one you like. If you know how to use trace paper as an overlaying system, then you probably don't need to read this chapter. Just use the planning ideas and the furniture standards in the other chapters as your guide.

for the Computer Whiz

A number of drafting programs are available for doing what I have described above on computer instead of by hand. You may already have a drawing application or you can purchase one. They are not very expensive.

The advantage to using a computer to draw a plan is that you can move the furniture pieces around very easily to form new room configurations. You can keep adding information as you go along. Also, some programs actually have a library of existing furniture, which can be selected and dropped right into your background drawing. After a brief learning curve, you will be amazed at how fast you can create a layout.

Some of these applications also have three-dimensional features, which give you the added advantage of seeing your new home office in perspective.

Sample Sketches

Figures 5-1 through 5-3 are sample sketches that should be helpful to you, serving as models for your own sketches. Sketch 5-3 has been duplicated on a computer (Figure 5-4), using a simple drafting software program, which may be purchased directly from the manufacturer. This program is one of those discussed above, able to project your plan into three-dimensions; these projections may be viewed from several angles. One example is shown in Figure 5-5.

Whichever method of layout you choose, putting something on paper is the surest way to get good planning results.

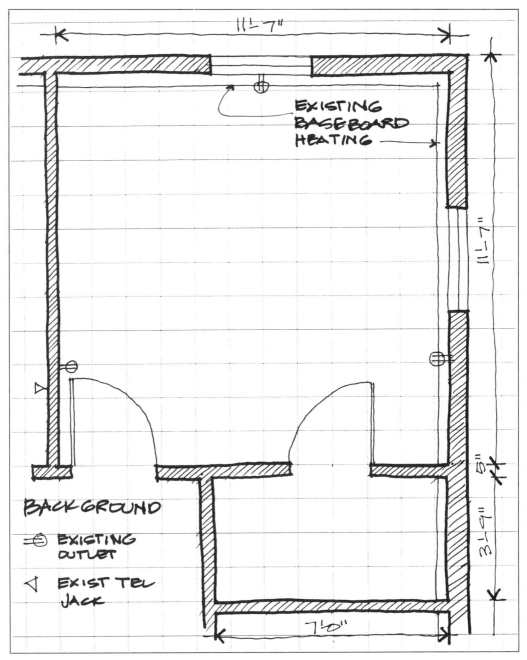

Figure 5-1
Sample room background sketch (no scale).

Courtesy of Bianco ■ Giolitto Architects, Middletown, CT.

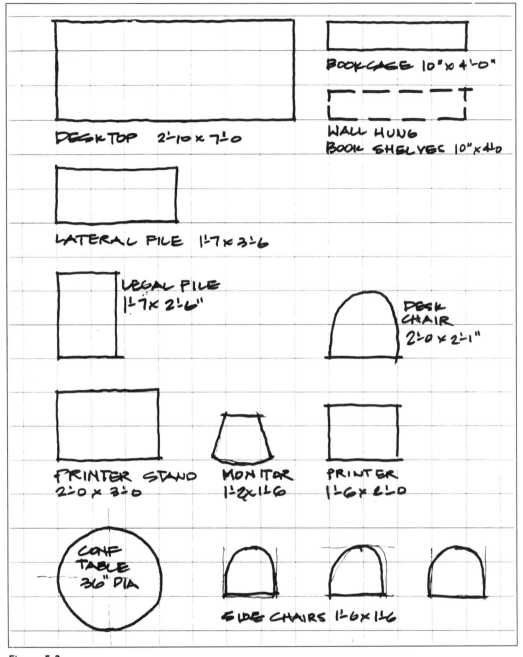

Figure 5-2
Sample furniture cutout sheet (no scale).

Courtesy of Bianco ■ Giolitto Architects, Middletown, CT.

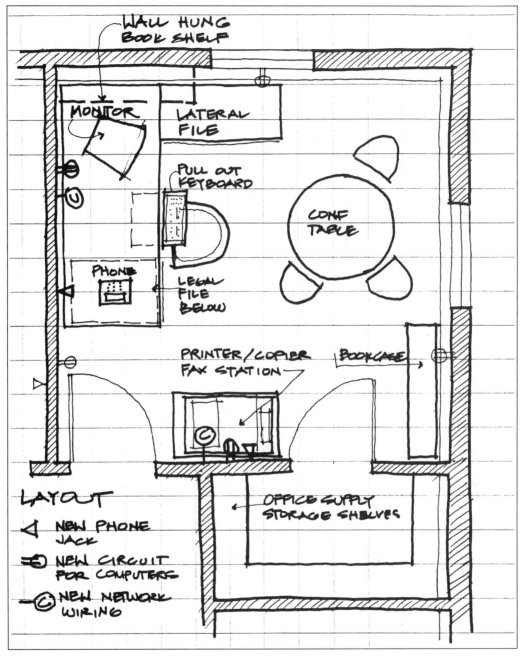

Figure 5-3
Furniture and power layout (no scale).
Courtesy of Bianco ■ Giolitto Architects, Middletown, CT.

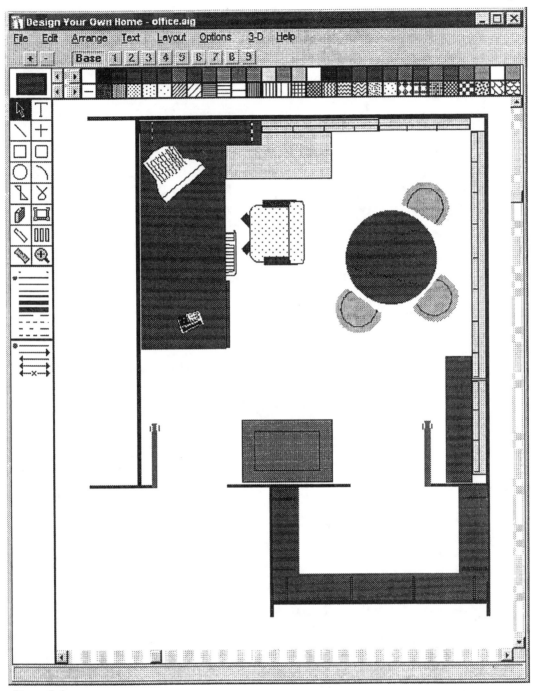

Figure 5-4
Home office plan, computer generated using "Design Your Own Home 3-D Walkaround."
Courtesy of Abracadata, Ltd., Eugene, OR.

Figure 5-5
Home office perspective view, computer generated using "Design Your Own Home 3-D Walkaround."
Courtesy of Abracadata, Ltd., Eugene, OR.

Results   You may find that you have room left over in your new home office—that's great! On the other hand, you may find that all your desk surfaces just won't fit, at which time you will be faced with deciding among the following alternatives:

1. Eliminate one or two surfaces by "doubling up" use. This will mean more work for you each time you have to clear a desk for a new task.

2. Perform some tasks in another location in the house.

3. Allocate a little more space in the room by eliminating nonoffice furniture.

4. Conserve space by "nesting" some furnishings when they aren't in use, to save on floor space. This may require some special purchases, but it is a great way to conserve on space. Closeted offices in armoires or wall units are basically nested units (see Chapter 7).

SPACE COSTS	DESCRIPTION	EST COST
PARTITIONING		
DOORS/WINDOWS		
CEILING LIGHTING		
AIR CONDITIONING		
HEATING		
PLUMBING		
INSULATION		
ELECTRICAL		
TELEPHONE CABLING		
PAINTING		
FLOORING		
WOODWORK/CABINETRY		
	TOTAL SPACE COSTS:	
FURNITURE COSTS		
WORKSTATION 1		
WORKSTATION 2		
WORKSTATION 3		
CONFERENCE		
STORAGE		
TASK CHAIRS		
CONFERENCE CHAIRS		
TASK LIGHTS		
ACCESSORIES		
ART		
	TOTAL FURNITURE COSTS:	
EQUIPMENT COSTS		
COMPUTERS		
PRINTERS		
COPIER		
FAX		
MODEM		
UPS		
PHONE SYSTEM		
ANS MACHINE		
RADIO/STEREO		
	TOTAL EQUIPMENT COSTS:	
	TOTAL COSTS:	

Figure 5-6
Budget control worksheet.

What's It All Gonna Cost?

All the planning in the world isn't worth a nickel if you can't afford the resulting design. That's why we've included the budget control worksheet in Figure 5-6 as a final step in the process. This checklist and budget form has line items that may not be applicable to your specific plans. You also may have some equipment and other items already. That's great! Just check 'em off, and go onto the next line.

A budget is only an estimate, and an estimate is only as good as the accuracy of the estimator. When you are budgeting for line item equipment, be certain that you can get what you want within your budget. In other words, you have to do some preliminary investigating.

If any construction is involved, now is the time to call in a contractor for an estimate. You have a floor plan, and you know exactly what you want to do. That's half the battle. If you compare contractor prices, they will be giving you an estimate on the same work. If your project involves a substantial amount of construction, *stop now*! Proceed directly to Chapter 13, Renovations, Additions, and New Construction.

As for furniture and accessories, there is a directory of contributors at the back of the book. If there is something you see in one of the chapters that you like, you can use the directory to locate a dealer in your area. In this way, you can get an idea of cost.

This concludes the planning work. What follows is considered by many to be the fun part—selecting furnishings for your very own personalized space. But before we dive headlong into looking at products, I thought it'd be a good idea to look at some basic ergonomic factors, and how they should affect your purchasing and planning decisions.

CHAPTER SIX
ERGONOMICS

User in upright position in the Jefferson chair.
Courtesy of the Alma Group, Elkhart, IN.

I DECIDED THAT IF I WERE GOING TO WRITE about ergonomics, I ought to be able to define it. So I looked it up in Webster's Third World Dictionary, which defines ergonomics as "biotechnology." Well, even if I can't offer you a clear and simple definition of ergonomics, at least I know what it is when I see it.

Compare ergonomics to wearing a shoe. If the shoe doesn't fit properly, it can be a very painful, even injurious experience. It often doesn't hurt right away, either. Otherwise you wouldn't have bought the shoe in the first place, right?

What it comes down to is that if you are sitting in one place for a long time, or doing a repetitive task, you may develop fatigue, discomfort, strain, and even personal injury. An ergonomic feature is designed to prevent those things from happening.

Back and leg pain, neck aches, eyestrain, and carpal tunnel syndrome are all real and unpleasant. As medical history develops around prolonged use of computers and other sedentary activities in the office, we have learned about workplace injury, as well as how to reduce the risk of it.

It used to be that when you worked for a large company, you were issued a desk and a chair, same for everybody. Now, concerned about the health of their employees and the risk of lawsuits, companies are hiring ergonomists, and purchasing specialized furnishings to reduce the risk of workplace injury.

You stand no lesser risk of workplace injury working home. But unlike the situation in a corporate office, it's your responsibility at home to select furniture that's just right for you.

Safety and Comfort versus Cost

Most people who begin to work at home are worried about the success of their new venture. It may be a new business, or simply a corporate telecommuting experiment. With risk comes caution, and that translates into "let's not buy anything I don't absolutely need."

People will sometimes spend a fortune on stationery or an elaborate computer system, but at the same time they are loathe to spend money on furniture. To reduce startup costs, they "make do" with a card table, or sit on a folding chair that they brought in from the garage. Cardboard boxes become the home office file cabinets.

The worry about starting something new and different is understandable, especially for any of us who have gone through it. Nevertheless, your health and comfort will have an affect on your productivity and ultimate success. If you are working uncomfortably, or if you injure yourself inadvertently, you will pay for it in lost income or opportunity.

Like everything else in life, there is a broad range of choices and costs associated with selecting furniture and equipment for an office. However, spending a large sum of money doesn't guarantee that you will get something that is either ergonomically "correct," or appropriate for you.

Alternatively, there are many fine products that have been brought to market during the last few years that are not only well-designed for comfort and safety, but are also reasonably priced.

You Can't Tell a Book by Its Cover

Don't be fooled by the visual appearance of a piece of furniture. For instance, a soft, overpadded chair may look inviting, and when you sit in it for the first few moments, it may feel comfortable and soothing. Over an eight hour workday, however, this chair may not support your back well, or may not move with you as your body turns, twists, and tilts from task to task.

The same holds true for a desk. It may look grand, and sport a hardwood finish that perfectly fits your decor. But the table surface may be too high, the drawers wrong for your filing needs, the knee space too narrow, and so on.

Choosing the Right Equipment for You

Before you even consider buying a piece of furniture or accessory, consider the following:

1. Nothing can be all things to all people. No two people are made the same, so why should we expect one size to fit all?

2. Depending on the tasks that we are performing, we may need different types and/or arrangements of furniture.

3. Just because a piece of furniture is adjustable, doesn't necessarily mean that it can adjust to your task and personal needs.

A good match means that the person, the tasks to be performed, and the design of the furniture work together in three-part harmony.

Ergonomics and Computers

Personal computers typically find their way onto work surfaces that were really made for writing or conferencing. We have come to learn that monitor and keyboard positions should vary based on the physical attributes of the user. Some manufacturers have developed workstations with a variety of built-in adjustments, specifically for computer use (see Chapter 7). Many manufacturers are now making retrofit items for standard-height work surfaces, which allow the user to adjust VDT and keyboard positions, relative to their individual needs (see Chapter 10, Ergonomic Tools).

Prescriptions for Comfort at the Computer

The following recommendations for posture and positioning have been supplied by Ergonomic Logic, Inc. of Sparks, Nevada, a manufacturer of ergonomic equipment for computer workstations:

- Sit squarely in front of the monitor and keyboard.
- Avoid twisting your neck and/or your body during data entry.
- Hands and wrists should be in a flat/level position relative to the floor.
- Avoid bending wrists up/down or to either side.
- The tips of the elbows should be level with the home row of the keyboard.
- The upper arms should be down at the sides of the torso.
- The angle between the upper arm and the forearm should not be less than 90 degrees or greater than 110 degrees.
- The angle between the torso and the thighs should not be less than 90 degrees or greater than 110 degrees. A slouched position (less than 90 degrees between the torso and the thigh, which causes compression of the lumbar spine and the body organs, should always be avoided.
- Thighs should be parallel to the floor.
- Avoid pressure on the back of the thighs by using an adjustable footrest.

- Due to the variety of body shapes and sizes, the computer operator chair should be adjustable. An elevated adjustable footrest may be necessary to accomplish a correct typing posture.
- Position the top of the monitor or CRT screen at eye level or lower and at a distance of approximately 18 to 24 inches away.

Helpful Charts and Other Information

We've included some nifty diagrams that will help you to make better decisions when purchasing or planning workstations, or buying seating. Figure 6-1 demonstrates the variety of seating adjustments that are available. Figure 6-2 reviews one of the most common repetitive stress injuries (RSI's) in Canada and the United States. Figure 6-3 discusses how to better organize your personal workspace to reduce potential discomfort and injury.

Also included are a handful of products, shown in Figure 6-4, that are designed to reduce workstation-related fatigue. This is only a small sampler, but it will hopefully give you a sense of what to think about, and what is available, especially when you start looking at workstation furniture and seating, in the following two chapters.

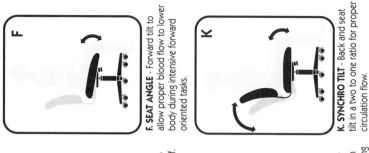

A. TILT TENSION - Increase or decrease the resistance of chair tilt.
B. INFINITE TILT LOCK - Lock chair in any tilt position for greatest comfort.

C. PNEUMATIC SEAT HEIGHT - Adjust until thighs and lower legs form a 90° angle.

D. BACK HEIGHT - Set the lumbar support to the most comfortable lower back supported position.

E. SEAT BACK DEPTH - Adjust for maximum comfort and support so front of seat is just behind the calf.

F. SEAT ANGLE - Forward tilt to allow proper blood flow to lower body during intensive forward oriented tasks.

G. BACK ANGLE - Adjust for optimum support, so lumbar cushion rests comfortably against lower back.

H. ARM HEIGHT - Adjust to maintain a proper 90° supported elbow angle.

I. ARM ANGLE - When tilting seat adjust to maintain a proper 90° supported elbow angle.

J. KNEE TILT - Recline with greater ease while allowing feet to remain comfortably on the floor enhancing circulation through lower body.

K. SYNCHRO TILT - Back and seat tilt in a two to one ratio for proper circulation flow.

Figure 6-1
Various ergonomic adjustments for seating.
Courtesy of Global Industries, Inc., Marlton, NJ

Making the task at hand - comfortable

Work Shouldn't Cause Pain

Speed, accuracy and productivity have become watch
words in business today. The blending of high technology in the office and factory environment has created workplaces where repetitive motions are commonplace for many.

The computerized office does not demand that people get up as often as was required just a
few years ago. A large portion of task oriented information is now filed electronically, for
instant recall on computer screens.

Repetitive Strain Injuries or RSIs are a
general class of disorders resulting from
strain to shoulders, arms, hands and
sometimes the back. RSI is also
referred to as Overuse Syndrome.

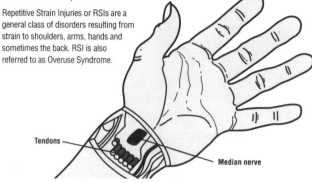

Tendons

Median nerve

TYPICAL RSI

Carpal Tunnel Syndrome is one of the most common
RSIs in Canada and United States. Repetitive motion
injuries are considered a job-related injury. There are nine
flexor tendons which are trapped in an unyielding fibre
and bone tunnel in the wrist. These tendons may
become irritated when your hands are held at an
awkward angle during long periods of repetitive use such
as data entry. If the tendons become inflamed and
swollen, the median nerve is compressed and numbness,
tingling and pain result.

RSI PREVENTION

A well designed ergonomic chair will assist you in achiev-
ing proper orientation of the arms, wrists and back. The
Global exclusive height adjustable arms, with optional
soft urethane pivotal arm rests (Pat. Pending) will help
you reach a level of unmatched comfort and support

ARM HEIGHT ADJUSTABILITY

Anthropometric (human form) data indicates that the elbow height range variation of the
average seated person is approximately 2.25 inches (57.15mm).

With the Global adjustable arm you can choose, with the push of a button, one of five
comfort zone heights. Additional width between armrests is available by adjusting four
screws easily accessed on the underside of the seat.

Arm ajustability a
desired feature

Different work
assignments, along
with body sizes
make us all unique

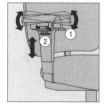
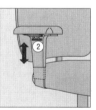

ADJUSTMENTS MADE EASY

Height adjustable and height/tilt adjustable arms are compatible with several Global
models. These arms are available with upholstered or self-skinned urethane arm caps.

Height/tilt adjustable arms # "I" and "J" allow the user to tilt the armrest forward or rearward.

Height adjustable arms on models # "H" and "D" allow the user to adjust arm height to
five levels.

① Arm tilt adjustment

② Arm height adjustment

FOOTROCKER

The FOOTROCKER helps to prevent possible discomfort resulting from outstretched
feet. A natural foot position can be assumed in a variety of seated tasks.

The rocking motion creates light activity in the legs and feet and will help stimulate
muscles to improve overall circulation.

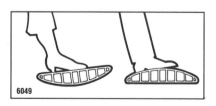

6049

Your Workplace

The Primary Workspace is the area swept by arm motions pivoting at the elbow with slight shoulder movement and no upper body twisting. This main area is used for a variety of basic tasks including writing, reading and computer work. The size or span of the primary workspace should complement the task being performed.

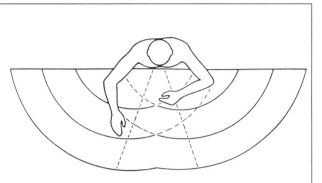

Consider the flow of work through your workstation in a typical day; you'll find a number of distinctive and repetitive task patterns. However, since the work patterns which your daily activities generate are sometimes too obvious to be recognized easily, the following chart will help to give you some ideas on improving your workspace.

THINGS TO CONSIDER	POSSIBLE CONCERNS	SOLUTIONS
tasks requiring computer use for extensive periods	fatigue and discomfort from constantly sitting in the same position	teach yourself to take small rest breaks. stretch your muscles and adjust your chair for a fresh posture position
handling and processing of a large amount of paper	repetitive un-natural twisted reaching could cause repetitive strain injuries	organize your primary work area to include the paper flow: additional desk tray organizers may be a cost-effective solution
do you have to leave your seating position often during the day to complete tasks?	strain of back muscles, if you are carrying stacks of paper	your work station should have enough room for you to easily move from and return to your main work surface area. a chair with arms will help you ease in and out of your work position
is your workstation used by more than you alone?	your work habits and personal body size may be quite different from those of the person you share with	make sure all furnishing are easily adjusted to suit the needs of both parties
do you use a pointing device, such as a mouse?	overuse of the mouse and awkward posture could bring on repetitive strain injuries	make sure you have a comfortable and stable platform for your pointing device (mouse). and your chair has arms for additional support
extensive use of the telephone during keystroking or writing	fatigue due to holding the phone handset and operating a keyboard at the same time	use a hands-free telephone or a phone headset which will allow you to maintain a normal posture while operating your computer
light sources need to be controlled to benefit your work environment	eye fatigue over a day will affect your well-being and productivity	use window blinds which can be adjusted throughout the day; install an anti-glare screen on your computer

Poorly designed or improperly adjusted office furniture can cause discomfort. Understanding your work flow and daily deadlines will help you organize a comfortable ergonomic work space. With proper knowledge of the capabilities of today's modern furniture, individualized comfort can be achieved, thus greatly affecting your level of comfort and productivity.

Ergonomics a better way of life

Figure 6-3
Ergonomic workspace organization.
Courtesy of Global Industries, Inc., Marlton, NJ.

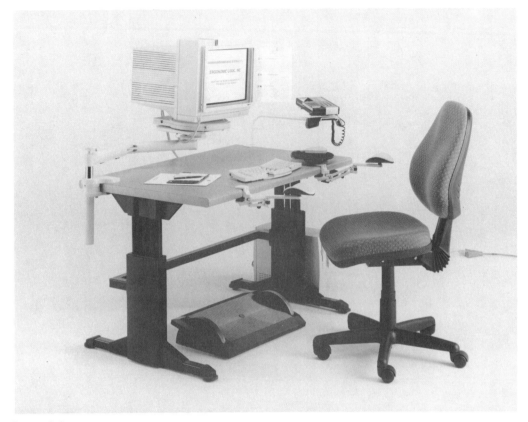

Figure 6-4
Ergonomic Logic, Inc. specializes in providing products that transdorm your existing nonadjustable workstation into a completely adjustable working environment. By accessorizing and adapting your existing working station, you can build ergonomic flexibility. Shown are ELI's task chair, mouse pad, footrest, monitor and phone stand, and articulating arm support.
Courtesy of Ergonomic Logic, Inc., Sparks, NV.

CHAPTER SEVEN
WORKSTATION FURNITURE

Detail of drop-leaf hardwood work table, one component of the TD system,
from the TD Collection.
Herman Miller for the Home, Zeeland, MI. Photo by Elliot Kaufman Photography.

THE COLLECTION OF INFORMATION ON WORKSTATIONS has been, for me, one of the most interesting parts of preparing this book.

I have mentioned previously that I consider the workstation to be the heart of the working office. It's been fun to see the broad variety of systems that furniture designers have developed for computer workstations and for home office use.

This chapter highlights some of these wonderful new and innovative products.

In the following pages, I will make specific comments about the products shown, but first I have a few general thoughts about workstation furniture, which I offer below.

Desks A desk is basically an administrative workstation. Most people read mail, write checks, and organize their time and paperwork at a desk. It is a good idea to have a phone at or near the desk, even if most of your calling and answering is done at the computer station.

Desks are not that suitable for project stations because of limited layout space, and because project work that used to be done at a desk is now often produced at a computer.

Desks normally contain storage below the work surface, for filing of records and storage of small office tools. If your desk is against a wall, then you can use shelving at the back of the desk or on the wall to hold your filing and tool storage.

File storage in a desk is advantageous for quick reference. When you open a drawer, you will be looking down at the top of your files, where it is easier to see labels on the tabs. Drawers offer your records a level of protection from dust, or from potential damage. When the drawers are closed, storage is concealed, thereby offering a neat and attractive appearance.

Tables Tables are ideal for meeting stations, because they have knee space below. Tables can be used for project stations, administrative stations, and, with the proper accessories, they can be converted into good computer workstations.

If your need for a project station varies, you may want to consider a table with collapsible legs, that can be set up for short duration and then stored away, adding floor space back to your home office.

Work Surface Heights

A practical table height for writing or conferencing is between 29 and 31 inches. The variation is based on personal preference. You will find that most table heights will finish at around 30 inches.

Other office equipment may be placed on counters as high as 36 inches, which is the typical height for kitchen counters. Some items, such as a large format copying machine, will be too high for comfortable use if placed on a 36 inch counter. Other equipment, such as a coffee maker, stapler, or scale, may be more convenient on a 36 inch counter. Thirty-six-inch-high counters have the advantage of providing storage below, but are too high for sitting work in a typical chair.

Traditional Desk–Credenza Arrangements

If you are going to seat visitors in pull-up chairs in front of your desk, you may want to consider a credenza behind you. The credenza can hold a telephone and other desktop elements, thereby freeing up the desktop surface. It can also hold a computer station arrangement.

In situations where people have credenzas or other work surfaces behind them, they may opt for a work surface in front (desktop) that is open below (no drawers or pedestals), thereby allowing visitors to pull up fully to the work surface, to closely review plans or other material. In this case, a conference-type table is doubling as a desk surface. A very popular choice for this arrangement is the "racetrack" shape, which allows as many as four people to pull up comfortably to the surface. Remember, however, that this type of surface, when used as a table, doesn't provide the visual screen that a desk with drawers or a modesty panel offers.

Computer Stations

Several manufacturers are producing computer workstations with a variety of adjustments for screen, keyboard, and mouse positioning. If you are setting up a computer workstation, you should definitely consider one of these units.

If you are going to work on a standard desk or table, you should consider getting ergonomic accessories which mount to the surface. See Chapter 6, Ergonomics, and Chapter 10, Ergonomic Tools.

Multifunction and Hideaway Stations

Recognizing that there is often a shortage of space in a home office, several manufacturers have developed fold-away offices, in armoires and wall units. When fully open, they often provide a combination of work surfaces and storage possibilities. When closed, they hide the office environment, and their face panels, which look like fine furniture, complement the room in which they are installed.

Ready-to-Assemble Furniture

A substantial portion of workstation furniture made today is shipped to the retailer unassembled, in flat boxes. This saves money that would otherwise be spent on factory assembly, shipment, storage, and reduces potential damage along the way. The savings are passed along to you, the buyer.

Ready-to-assemble (RTA) furniture does not automatically mean inferior quality. In fact, manufacturers have been making RTA workstations for the finest corporate offices for decades. As in any business, there are Chevrolets and Cadillacs, and some lemons too.

If you buy brand-name furniture from a reputable dealer, you shouldn't have any problems. And if you run into a snag, a good company will support you to get the problem solved. A number of products presented in this chapter are sold RTA.

Furniture Finishes

The choice of finish is largely a matter of preference and budget, but you should also consider wear.

Laminated surfaces are generally less expensive than real wood veneers. Real wood surfaces make a statement, however, that can't be overlooked when you are considering visitors.

People used to place clear glass on the tops of their desks to protect the wood desktop surface. If you wish to protect the top of your desk, there are many other accessories and protective surfaces that are now available.

Considering All Factors

If you have read the chapters on planning and carefully determined your workstation requirements, you will be better prepared to make comparisons. Don't be overimpressed by appearance or cost. Be sure that what you buy will be functional for your needs.

Cost Range Code

Below each caption you will notice a horizontal group of diamonds, one of which is blackened. As the blackened diamond moves from left to right, comparative costs rise. *This is a cost-range code only, and its purpose is to give you a general sense of price* relative to similar products or manufacturers. Notice that there is no specific price attached to any of the diamonds or ranges. Prices will vary based on configurations and finishes chosen. Also, dealer pricing varies widely and changes regularly. You can, however, obtain specific pricing on any workstation shown in this book by calling the phone numbers listed for each provider in the Directory of Contributors.

Laptop Roll-Abouts

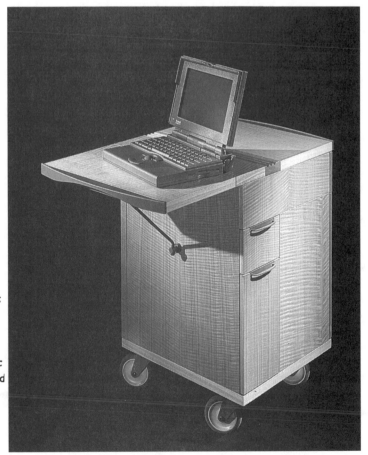

Figure 7-1
Knoll System 6—
Companion is a stand-alone, portable work surface and storage unit designed specifically for laptop computers. Great storage; with the top folded away, it can double as a bedside stand. Available in plastic laminate colors and wood veneers.
Courtesy of The Knoll Group,
New York, NY
◇◇◆◇◇

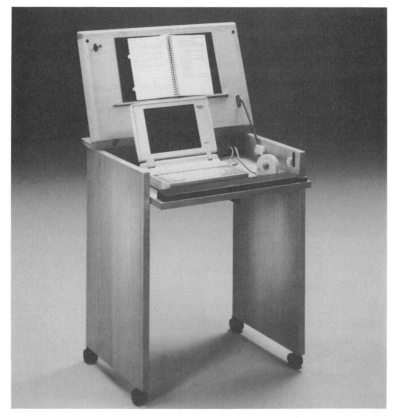

Figure 7-2
Nucraft Notebook Computer Cart is an alternative to the much larger computer furniture pieces designed for desk-based computers. Locking casters, and lock away top; built-in palm rest and wire management. Available in oak, walnut, or maple.
Courtesy of Nucraft Furniture Company, Comstock Park, MI.
✧✧✧◆✧✧

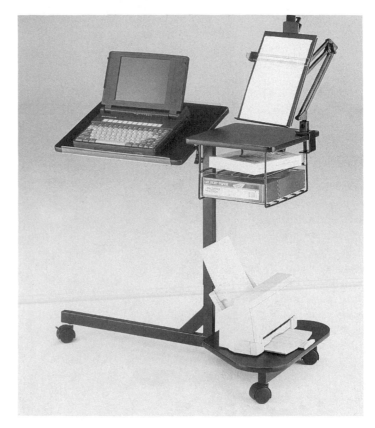

Figure 7-3
Balt Lapmaster is a really nifty notebook cart. Great for normal seating, or even for use in bed. Includes adjustable paper holder, writing surface, supplies, printer spot, and adjustable notebook tablet; locking casters.
Courtesy of Balt, Inc., Cameron, TX.
✧✧◆✧✧✧

Accessory Workstations

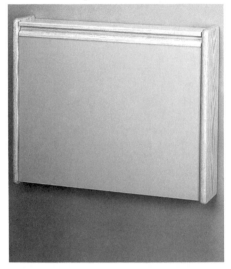

(a) (b)

Figure 7-4
Peter Pepper Products' Express Desk is a wall-mounted workstation that can be used near a desk as a laptop side station, or in a pinch, as extra lay or writing space. (a) It takes up no floor space; with the smooth, glide-down door closed, it protrudes only 4 inches from the wall. (b) Open, it provides extra space as shown. Variety of wood finishes, interior storage compartments.
Courtesy of Peter Pepper Products, Inc., Compton, CA.
❖❖◆❖❖

Mobile Computer Stations

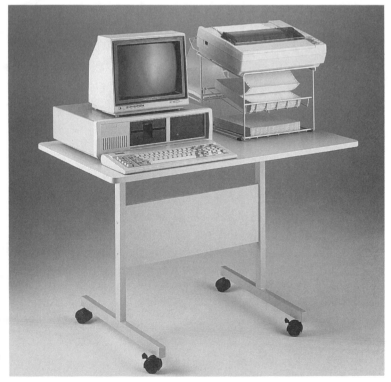

Figure 7-5
Balt Company produces a variety of sturdy and flexible mobile workstations, like this one. In tight quarters, one of these can be the answer to your entire computer station needs, leaving room for project and administrative stations.
Courtesy, Balt, Inc., Cameron, TX.
❖❖◆❖❖

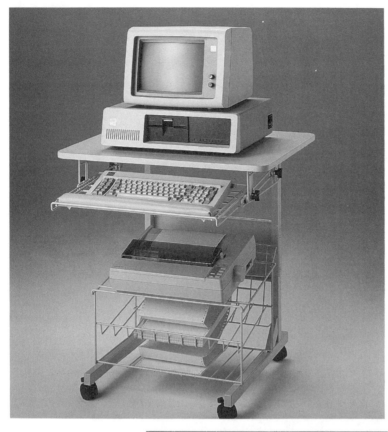

Figure 7-6
**Another Balt Company
mobile workstation.
This one includes an
adjustable keyboard
tray.**

Courtesy, Balt, Inc.,
Cameron, TX.
✧✧◆✧✧

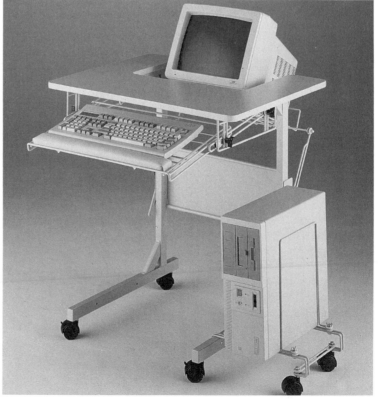

Figure 7-7
**Another Balt Company
mobile workstation.**

Courtesy, Balt, Inc., Cameron, TX.
✧✧◆✧✧

Design-Your-Own Component Workstations

Figure 7-8
The Container Store helps you to build your own workstation arrangement by selecting individual components that suit your needs and space constraints. Simple units for work surfaces, pedestals for storage, and wall-mounted shelving can all be integrated for a unified appearance.
Courtesy of Container Store®, Dallas, TX
✧✧◆✧✧✧

Figure 7-9
Another arrangement of components.
Courtesy of Container Store®, Dallas, TX
✧✧◆✧✧✧

Figure 7-10
Another of the many desk configurations that can be organized with parts available through The Container Store.
Courtesy of Container Store®, Dallas, TX
✧✧◆✧✧✧

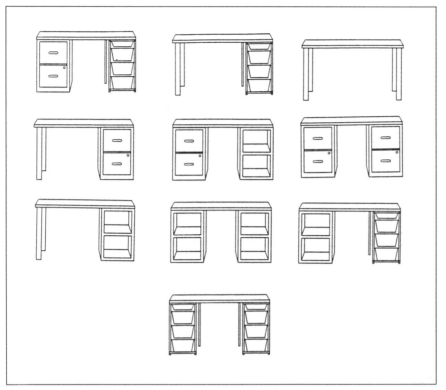

Figure 7-11
Container Store's System offers a variety of pedestal configurations.

Courtesy of Container Store®, Dallas, TX
✧✧◆✧✧

Figure 7-12
AnthroCarts are a favorite of mine, because they are sturdy, flexible, modular, mobile, relatively child-safe, and can be customized to your liking. Configurations are almost limitless.

Courtesy of Anthro Corporation, Tualatin, OR.
✧✧✧◆✧✧

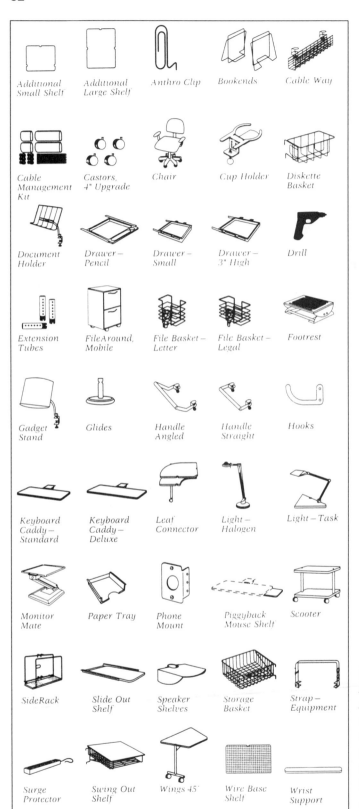

Figure 7-15
Accessories for 24-inch-wide AnthroCarts. There is hardly anything Anthro hasn't thought of to help you completely deck out your workstation.
Courtesy of Anthro Corporation, Tualatin, OR.
✧✧✧✦✧✧

Ready-to-Assemble (RTA) Panel Workstations

Figure 7-16
This two-tone station
by 3K Möbel serves two
purposes:
administrative and
meetings. Pedestals are
free to roll out from
under, making for a
larger meeting table,or
project station.
Courtesy of 3K Möbel, Irvine, CA.
✧✧✧◆✧✧

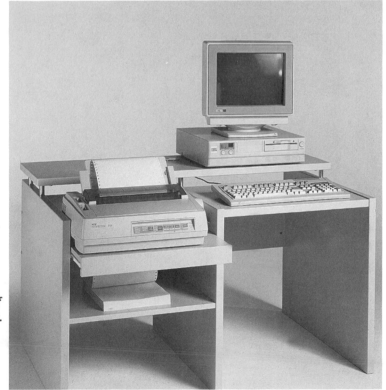

Figure 7-17
Basic tiered workstation
with roll-out printer shelf
and paper storage below.
Also available in two
colors.
Courtesy of 3K Möbel, Irvine, CA.
✧◆✧✧✧

Figure 7-18
One of many furniture ensembles offered by 3K Möbel, includes storage units, drawers, movable pedestals, dropped keyboard surface.

Courtesy of 3K Möbel, Irvine, CA.
◇◇◇◆◇◇

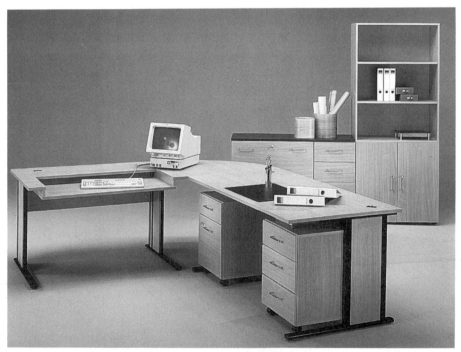

Figure 7-19
Wood-grain style finish with black accents; notice grommets for wire management.

Courtesy of 3K Möbel, Irvine, CA.

◇◇◇◆◇◇

Figure 7-20
This contemporary L-shaped unit from 0'Sullivan's Scandinavian collection has several nice features for computer use, and doubles nicely as a computer station/administrative station. Rounded surface edges and Euro-styled drawer pulls are nice added touches. Lots of storage, too.
Courtesy of O'Sullivan Industries, Inc., Lamar, MO.
✧✧◆✧✧

Figure 7-21
Details show CPU storage, pull-out printer drawer, and keyboard.
Courtesy of O'Sullivan Industries; Lamar, MO.

Figure 7-22
This computer credenza features a sturdy pull-out keyboard shelf with a comfort rail and a pull-out mouse shelf.
Courtesy of O'Sullivan Industries, Inc., Lamar, MO.
✧◆✧✧✧

Figure 7-23
The computer credenza can be expanded with a hutch, an adjacent file cabinet, and an executive desk with a modesty panel, and drawer configurations.
Courtesy of O'Sullivan Industries, Inc., Lamar, MO.
✧✧◆✧✧

Figure 7-24
**O'Sullivan's Cockpit work center allows
the operator to adopt and maintain a
reclined posture and provides support for
the arms while working; built in angled
foot rest.**
Courtesy of O'Sullivan Industries, Inc., Lamar, MO.
✧✧◆✧✧

Figure 7-25
**Overhead view of the Cockpit shows how
shelving and storage spaces are within
arm's reach; work surface tilts up to assist
arm support.**
Courtesy of O'Sullivan Industries, Inc., Lamar, MO.

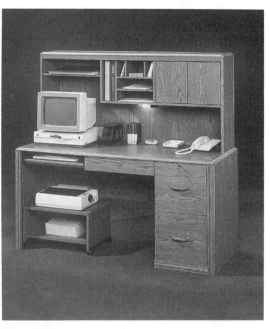

Figure 7-26
Sauder's Computer Cart, on casters, is stacked high, but only 25 inches wide. Mouse shelf extends left or right.
Courtesy of Sauder Woodworking; Archbold, OH.
✧◆✧✧✧✧

Figure 7-27
This office work center provides both administrative and computer space in one unit, with a roll-out printer stand below. Drawers have full extension slides and hold legal or letter size files.
Courtesy of Sauder Woodworking; Archbold, OH.
✧◆✧✧✧✧

Figure 7-28
Dark wood and classic pulls give this computer/administrative station a very traditional appearance. Pencil drawer front converts to pull-out keyboard shelf. Hidden mouse shelf and printer paper shelf behind drawers.
Courtesy of Sauder Woodworking; Archbold, OH.
✧◆✧✧✧✧

Figure 7-29
Home Depot's
Norcraft home office
environment presents a
custom appearance
using an arrangement
of Norcraft cabinets,
available through any
of their stores.

Courtesy of The Home Depot.
Photo by Paul Johnson.
✧✧◆✧✧

U-Shaped Workstations

Figure 7-30
Example of a U-shaped desk configuration, which provides computer, administrative, meeting, and
project stations all in one. From the Roma collection.
Courtesy of Global Industries, Inc. Marlton, NJ.
✧✧◆✧✧

Figure 7-31
LA Z Boy's Nebula series
offers a wide variety of
workstation and storage
arrangements, from
which you may build one
or more coordinated
workstations for various
tasks.
Courtesy of LA Z Boy Business
Furniture, Monroe, MI.
❖❖◆❖❖

"Hideaway" Stations in Traditional Garb

Figures 7-32 (left) and 7-33 (right)
Hooker Furniture makes these beautiful armoire work centers in solid maple or cherry veneer.
They feature a pull-out keyboard tray and pull-out printer tray. Work surface drops down, creating
an L-shaped work area, which is very handy when working with a computer screen. A fine
workstation in a fine piece of furniture. Figure 7-33 shows the closed unit.
Courtesy of Hooker Furniture Corporation, Martinsville, VA.
❖❖❖◆❖

Figure 7-34
A computer station is
nicely worked into this
traditional roll-top
tambour desk. Figure
7-35 shows the desk
closed.
Courtesy of Hooker Furniture
Corporation, Martinsville, VA.
✧✧✧✦✧

Figure 7-35
The unit in Figure 7-34
above, closed.
Courtesy of Hooker Furniture
Corporation, Martinsville, VA.

Figure 7-36
Sligh Furniture Company offers traditional-style, multifunctional home office furniture that blends nicely into areas not reserved exclusively for work. Here, a traditional desk features a lockable center drawer that flips down to accommodate a keyboard. Right pedestal drawer facade is actually a hinged door that conceals storage and a pull-out printer drawer. Wire management and heat escapement also built-in.
Courtesy of Sligh Furniture Company, Holland, MI.
✧✧✧✧◆✧

Figure 7-37
The desk in Figure 7-36, with its special features showing.
Courtesy of Sligh Furniture Company, Holland, MI.

Figure 7-38
This roll-out credenza and pocket chair will warm any room. When the unit is closed, the pocket chair nests within the knee space.
Courtesy of Sligh Furniture Company, Holland, MI.
✧✧✧✧◆✧

Figure 7-39
The unit in Figure 7-38, opened to form an L-shaped computer station with pull-out keyboard tray and printer drawer.
Courtesy of Sligh Furniture Company, Holland, MI.

Figure 7-40
Sligh's Homeworks™
computer cabinet closes
into a fine wood hutch
that would grace
anyone's living quarters.
Courtesy of Sligh Furniture
Company, Holland, MI.
❖❖❖❖◆❖

Figure 7-41
The unit in Figure 7-40
with its bifold doors laid
back on its sides to
reveal a complete
closeted computer
station with terrific
functional appoint-
ments, including
keyboard trays, writing
slides, adjustable
shelves, and a roll-out
printer drawer. Wire
management is
concealed behind a
fabric covered
tackboard. Pocket
chair optional. Select
hardwood solids and
brass hardware. A
functional and esthetic
pleasure.
Courtesy of Sligh Furniture
Company, Holland, MI.

Figures 7-42 and 7-43
When closed, this unit acts as a handsome wall console. It can also quickly turn into an additional work surface. The console opens to provide an additional work surface.
Courtesy of Sligh Furniture Company, Holland, MI.
✧✧✧✧◆✧

Figure 7-44
What appears to be a traditional coffee table is actually a convertible table/desk. The top rises up and diagonally toward the user.
Courtesy of Sligh Furniture Company, Holland, MI.
✧✧✧✧◆✧

Figure 7-45
The "converted" unit is an excellent choice for a seating/meeting area, or for just plain relaxed work right on the couch.
Courtesy of Sligh Furniture Company, Holland, MI.

Offices "On the Move"

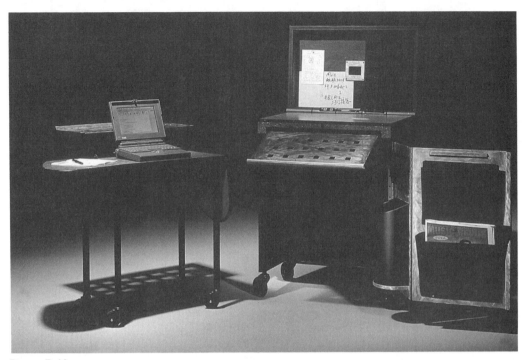

Figure 7-46
Haworth's 13-cubic-foot Office-in-a-Box unit is fully functional with electrical outlets, a phone jack, and a LAN port. All work utensils, personal materials, and works-in-process can be permanently left in the unit; when the box is closed up and not in use, items may be left on the work and reference surfaces, as well as in storage areas inside the lid, door, and main box cavity.
Courtesy of Haworth, Inc., Holland, MI.
❖❖❖◆❖

Figure 7-47
Closed view of Haworth's Office-in-a-Box.
Courtesy of Haworth, Inc., Holland, MI.

Figure 7-48
Haworth's "Steamer" draws its
inspiration and its name from a simpler
product created in a less complicated
era—the steamer trunk. It is apt to be
found in a satellite or home office for
telecommuting workers, or as a
temporary or addressable office for
workers requiring office space on a
sporadic basis. Features freestanding
work surface, adjustable height shelves
and work surfaces, and a left- or
right-hand locking door. The whole unit
can be moved on a two-wheel dolly.
Courtesy of Haworth, Inc., Holland, MI.
✧✧✧✦✧

Figure 7-49
A view of Haworth's "Steamer" in its
open position.
Courtesy of Haworth, Inc., Holland, MI.

Figure 7-50
Known as "Crossings," this Haworth furniture collection confronts the need for offices to be freely
arranged and adapted by individual users and teams in order that they might create environments
specific to their tasks. Although conceptualized for a collaborative workplace, this system's
flexibility makes it a worthy candidate for a single-user home office.
Courtesy of Haworth, Inc., Holland, MI.
✧✧✧✧◆✧

Figure 7-51
Another piece from Haworth's
"Crossings" collection.
Courtesy of Haworth, Inc., Holland, MI.

Figure 7-52
Turnstone's Docker desk and worktable has a flip-top rear door, which reveals storage and wire management for computer gear and other electronic equipment.
Photo courtesy of Steelcase, Inc., Grand Rapids, MI.
✧✧✧◆✧✧

Figure 7-53
Turnstone's Interactive desk gives you room for a computer, plus a couple of small drawers to stash everyday stuff. The 58 inch desk also has a removable pull-out shelf for truly comfortable keyboarding.
Photo courtesy of Steelcase, Inc., Grand Rapids, MI.
✧✧✧◆✧✧

Workstation Furniture Systems for the Home Office

Figure 7-54
Turnstone's U-shaped grouping shown here includes Interactive and Docker work tables, along with three (stackable) storage cabinets, one of which has two lateral file drawers. Available finished in melamine, veneer, or combination.
Photo courtesy of Steelcase, Inc., Grand Rapids, MI.
✧✧✧◆✧✧

Figure 7-55
Turnstone shows how to take a small space at home, and outfit it for a homey home office. Docker desk (with flipper door shown up), and two storage cabinets, stacked; one with doors, the other with lateral file drawers.
Photo courtesy of Steelcase, Inc., Grand Rapids, MI.
✧✧✧◆✧✧

Figure 7-56
Herman Miller developed the JB Collection specifically for appropriateness of scale, aesthetics and cost for the home, while also attending to work function and ergonomic features. Work surface edges are contoured. Electronics and wires are accommodated and managed easily. Shown here a variety of modules for task, storage, and filing, in an L-shaped configuration.
Courtesy of Herman Miller for the Home, Zeeland, MI. Photo by Nick Merrick, © Hedrich-Blessing
✧✧✧✦✧✧

Figure 7-57
Shown here a U-shaped configuration of the JB Collection with a corner computer station and a
vertical storage element; adjustable keyboard tray reduces the risk of repetitive stress injury.
Courtesy of Herman Miller for the Home, Zeeland, MI. Photo by Nick Merrick, © Hedrich-Blessing
✧✧✦✧✧

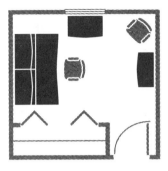
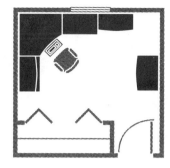

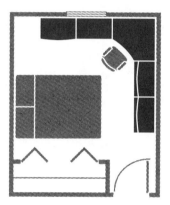
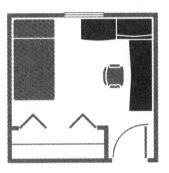

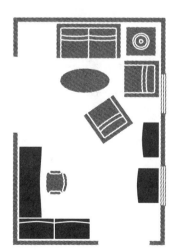
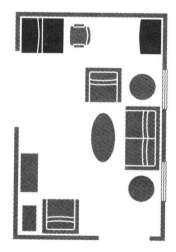

Figure 7-58
A variety of JB System configurations at home.
Courtesy of Herman Miller for the Home, Zeeland, MI.

Figure 7-59
The warmth of solid hardwood, along with graceful lines and careful detailing lets the TD collection stand on its own as a finely crafted, enduring design. When TD shares a family room, living area, or bedroom with other home furnishings, it doesn't interfere. Shown here is a corner computer station, with a project/administrative surface on one side, and a vertical storage/ filing unit on the other. Notice the tilted surfaces, excellent for input work.
Courtesy of Herman Miller for the Home, Zeeland, MI. Photo by Nick Merrick, © Hedrich-Blessing
✧✧✧✧♦✧

Figure 7-60
Another example of a configuration of the TD ensemble, this time with two vertical storage units. Notice the door storage section on one of the vertical units and the printer, neatly tucked away but accessible, on the lower shelf of the other vertical unit.
Courtesy of Herman Miller for the Home, Zeeland, MI.
✧✧✧✧✦✧

The Ultimate "Thinking Station"

Figure 7-61
This is not just another recliner—it is a unique marriage between seating and workstation that is unlike anything else currently on the market. The Alma Jefferson chair supports its occupant, in a variety of work positions from upright to reclining, by bringing the "work" to the user, set upon a variety of accessory support stands.
Courtesy of The Alma Group, Elkhart, IN.
✧✧✧✧✧✦

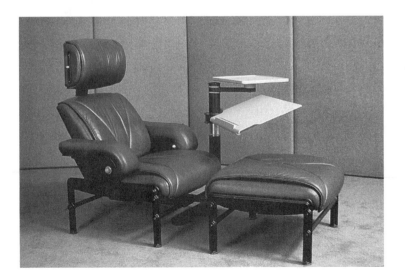

Figure 7-62
Side view of the Jefferson chair and ottoman.
Courtesy of The Alma Group, Elkhart, IN.

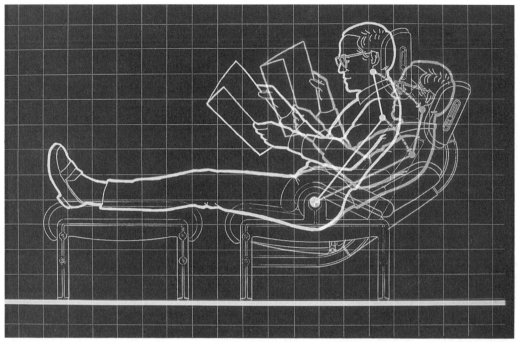

Figure 7-63
Central to the concept are the chair and the ottoman. The chair is suspended from a central point that is close to the natural pivoting action of the body. As a result, it provides superior head, torso and back support in a continuous range of upright and reclining positions.
Courtesy of The Alma Group, Elkhart, IN.

Figure 7-64
Easy access controls permit adjustment of the headrest, the neck support, and the back of the chair. The chair arms move in conjunction with the back. Firm padding relieves pressure on the body, and the ottoman supports the feet and legs.
Courtesy of The Alma Group, Elkhart, IN

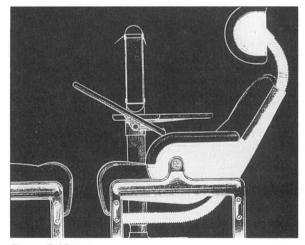

Figure 7-65
This profile demonstrates one of the accessories, the cantilever table and lamp, working in proximity to the Jefferson chair. A variety of accessories is available,
Courtesy of The Alma Group, Elkhart, IN

Ultimate Closeted Office

Figure 7-66
The Steelcase Personal Harbor
Workspace is a semienclosed
structure in which the user can
adjust a range of elements, including
work surfaces, lighting, ventilation,
and storage. It features acoustical,
visual and territorial privacy. It
occupies 48 square feet of space,
and is 78 inches high. Unit shown
here with semicircular lockable
sliding door closed.
Photo courtesy of Steelcase, Inc., Grand Rapids, MI.
✧✧✧✧✦

Figure 7-67
Another view of the Personal Harbor
Workspace with the sliding door
slightly open.
Photo courtesy of Steelcase, Inc., Grand Rapids, MI.

Figure 7-68
An interior view of the Personal Harbor Workspace. Based on column and beam architecture, it provides storage for technology and an electronic totem pole, to facilitate power access for personal devices, such as radios or CD players. The totem also contains two file drawers and two personal drawers. The product is offered with individual controls for lights, a fan and access to electrical power.
Photo courtesy of Steelcase, Inc., Grand Rapids, MI.

Figure 7-69
Another view of the
interior of the Personal
Harbor Workspace.
Photo courtesy of Steelcase, Inc.,
Grand Rapids, MI.

CHAPTER EIGHT
SEATING

Courtesy of The Knoll Group, New York, NY. Photo by Robert Kato

I BELIEVE THAT THE MOST IMPORTANT PIECE of furniture you will select for your office is your workstation chair. You may sit in it for over eight hours per day, every day. It supports your entire body. It affects your posture. And it affects your range of movement. As far as I'm concerned, a good chair will go a long way toward preventing back, neck, and other problems associated with long-term workstation use. You also don't have to "spend an arm and a leg" to get a decent chair.

How They Look versus How They Sit

Buyers may be tempted to purchase a chair because of its visual allure. Many chairs, especially of the overstuffed "executive" ilk, just don't offer proper anatomical support during prolonged sitting.

Even more confusing can be the initial feel of a chair. Upon first sitting, it may feel as if a particular chair is caressing your every body part This initial pleasurable feeling may be meaningless, however, from the point of view of long-term seating and anatomy. Pain associated with seating may develop slowly, often over many months or even years.

Your body and limbs, spine, and neck will be supported by and affected by the chair you sit in, all day every day. A well-designed chair will take the major body parts into account. Illustrations in Chapter 6 have demonstrated the variety of posture elements that are addressed by a properly planned chair. These are not gimmicks—office chair design has evolved over the last 100 years, based on the experience, discomfort, and injuries developed from the simple act of sitting still.

Chair Size and Anatomy

It is very important to choose a chair whose seat is sized correctly for your anatomy, so that you get the proper support of your legs, thighs, spine, arms and head. Pain caused by long-term use of improper seating can be very hard to diagnose.

There is no such thing as a chair that will work universally for all body sizes. That's why you have to choose the chair with the sizes and features that are right for you. You have to personally sit in the chair you buy. Whether you buy a chair from the corner store, or a mail-order company, be sure that you can return it for a refund or credit, if necessary, after a brief trial period. Seating is too personal to be purchased without the possibility of exchange.

Chair Adjustments

Adjustments on chairs are an important feature, especially for those used at computer workstations. Seat height, back height, and back support forward pressure are all important adjustments for your body, which you can reconfigure as your tasks change, or if you feel you simply need to reposition your body support within the chair during the course of a long workday.

A chair with a pneumatically adjustable seat height gives you the ability to adjust to the work surface height, but also affects your leg position relative to the floor. The lever adjustment allows you to quickly modify the height without having to get out of the chair.

The more adjustments, the more likely you will be able to adjust a chair to suit you. But you have to try it out. You will know very quickly whether the chair is sized properly for you. Remember that the adjustments should be used to fine tune body support, not to resize the chair.

Chair Bases

Office chairs now have what is referred to as a five-star base. That is to say, the stem that supports the seat sits on five radiating horizontal legs (like a starfish), usually with wheels (casters) at the tips.

Not too long ago, chairs had four-star bases. The problem with them was that if you were to tilt your body weight in just the wrong way, the chair would tip over, skate out from under you and spill you onto the floor. I'm giving away my age, but in the "old days," I was suddenly introduced to the floor by my (very expensive leather executive) chair, at least two times that I can remember. If you have (or are given) one of these four star relics, you would do well to get rid of it. It is an accident waiting to happen.

I think it's important for your workstation chair to be fitted with casters. You need to be able to move around within the locus of your workstation, to get to drawers, to reach to the back of the desk, and to reposition yourself at the right distance from your work surface or monitor.

Casters are useless, however, if they get bogged down on deep-pile carpets. Casters will also wear out low pile carpets quickly in the area of the chair base. It is a good idea to place a mat under the chair, to protect the carpet, and to help you glide more smoothly. There are a variety of mats available at office supply stores; some of them are transparent and will let the floor or carpet show through, fading into the background.

Leg Support

As the old song goes, "the leg bone's connected to the thigh bone," and so on. You can develop a pain in your back that is actually caused by improper leg support.

If your legs dangle from your seat (seat height too high), this can put pressure on your spine. Even though your legs may be planted on the floor, they still may pull on the spine and lower torso, which over time may cause back strain.

Leg support has come to be recognized as important for relieving pressure on the spine. That's why some chairs feature a vertically adjustable foot ring. By resting your feet on the ring, it will slightly elevate the legs, taking some pressure off of the spine. Another way to accomplish leg support is with an adjustable, tilting footrest, which sits on the floor, independent of the chair (see Chapter 10, Ergonomic Tools).

Thigh Support

When you are seated, your thighs are supported mostly by the forward edge of your chair seat. This can create a pressure point over time, restricting circulation. Fatigue and strain can be caused by pressure that the seat edge exerts on the thighs of the legs.

That's why many manufacturers curve, or "waterfall" the front edge of their chair seats. The waterfall relieves the hard front edge that creates thigh pressure. Many chair seats are designed to tilt forward from pressure at the front edge, bringing the entire body into a slightly thrust forward position, and relieving pressure on the thighs.

A seat that is too short from front to back will allow the thighs to "hang" over the front edge, which gives them no support and can also cause fatigue.

Arm Support

Chair arms have been receiving a lot of design attention lately. Similar to your legs, your arms hang off your torso, and all the weight gets transferred down through your spine. Think of your arms as you would tree branches. Chairs that can do some supporting of the arms, especially in conjunction with the use of computer keypads, will go a long way to alleviate tension, and reduce the pressure on the wrists that could contribute to carpal tunnel syndrome.

If a chair arm is adjustable, you can then position the height, and even the forward tilt of the arm, to work in combination with the height and location of your keyboard, thereby giving support to your forearms. You can also purchase armrests that attach to your work surface (see Chapter 10).

Spinal Support   If you were to view an x-ray profile of a person sitting in a chair, you would notice that the spine, which is doing all the supporting of the upper torso, like the trunk of a tree, is naturally curved and ends at a point in the pelvic area. You should look for a chair that has specific features, preferably adjustable, that address these support requirements.

There are chair backs made with adjustable tensioning devices, which will personalize the upper back support for your needs. Some chairs have pneumatic adjustments in the backrest, which will allow you to change back support pressure simply by pumping up, or releasing air in a chamber embedded in the backrest.

Some chair backs can be positioned vertically so that you can align the back piece to your physique for maximum spine support. Some chairs have an adjustment that allows the back to be moved closer to the front edge of the chair, or farther away. This is primarily a back-support pressure adjustment.

Headrests   Many chairs now being manufactured for office use come with adjustable headrests. These are different from the one-piece "executive" chairs, which are not adjustable and which can be quite uncomfortable for prolonged sitting. The high back of these executive chairs is unfortunately associated more with the user's status than with his or her well-being. A chair with an adjustable headrest, however, can allow the user to periodically rest the head by leaning back. Although this is not a preferred position for computing, it may be helpful while on the phone, or for short periods of rest. One of the most common aches at the end of a long hard day at office is a veritable "pain in the neck." It's hard to blame that pain on the boss if you are the boss.

Neck pains often come from the strain of attempting to support and maintain the head in a fixed position all day long. A headrest can provide for intermittent relaxation of the muscles that support the head, which will reduce the strain.

Flexibility and Body Movement

During the course of a business day, you move around a lot, sitting right in your chair. You answer the phone, you work on your computer, you roll over to the printer or to a file drawer. Your chair should have some flexibility, or the ability to move with you. The back should follow you forward, and allow you to relax by swaying backward. A seat that tilts forward as well as backward gives you an added dimension of flexibility and comfort.

Covering Materials

The coverings and material you choose will be mainly a personal matter, although it is important that the material be able to "breathe." Vinyl, for instance, is not particularly suitable for long-term sitting because it doesn't allow body sweat to escape, or evaporate. Even leather, which does breathe somewhat, may feel "sticky" to some people.

Whatever cover material you choose, be sure that it is a color or pattern you can live with, one that won't wear out quickly, or rapidly soil. You may find that it's more expensive to recover a chair than to buy a whole new chair.

Cost Range Code

Below each caption you will notice a horizontal group of diamonds, one of which is blackened. As the blackened diamond moves from left to right, comparative costs rise. *This is a cost-range code only, and its purpose is to give you a general sense of price* relative to similar products or manufacturers. Notice that there is no specific price attached to any of the diamonds or ranges. Prices will vary based on configurations and finishes chosen. Also, dealer pricing varies widely and changes regularly. You can, however, obtain specific pricing on any item shown in this book by calling the phone numbers listed for each provider in the Directory of Contributors.

Figure 8-1
Shown here is one of Global Industries many ergonomic task chairs, with pneumatic seat height, back height, and seat back depth adjustments. Global has an amazing variety of seating for all types, sizes, and budgets.
Courtesy of Global Industries, Inc., Marlton, NJ.
✧◆✧✧✧

Figure 8-2
Haworth's Accolade series, offered in both high-back and mid-back styles, with a variety of upholstery options, has a synchronized tilt mechanism, which enables the chair seat and back to articulate independently. The chairs also feature Back height adjustment, pneumatic or mechanical seat-height adjustments, six position back lock, forward-tilt mechanism, and adjustable task arms. They comply with American National Standard for Human Factors Engineering of Visual Display Terminal Workstations and with ANSI/BIFMA test standards.
Courtesy of Haworth, Inc., Holland, MI.
✧✧✧◆✧✧

Figure 8-3
*Turnstone's Poundcake series
provides cushions that shift
and conform to your shape.
All models include adjustable
recline tension and lock,
adjustable back height,
pneumatic height adjustment
and adjustable seat depth.
They are available in a variety
of fabric colors.*
Photo courtesy of Steelcase Inc.,
Grand Rapids, MI.
❖❖❖◆❖❖

Figure 8-4
*Equa 2 is an enhanced
version of one of Herman
Miller's best-selling seating
series. The chair is designed
to accommodate a broad
diversity of body types, and
large blocks of time spent at
computers. An optional
lumbar adjustment allows
user to inflate the chair back
for lower-back support. Arms
adjust for height, width, and
can be angled inward and
outward in a 25-degree
range to give task-intensive
computer users forearm
support while keyboarding or
mousing. The chair is now
available in three sizes,
offering even better fit,
comfort, and support.*
Courtesy of Herman Miller for the
Home, Zeeland, MI. Photo by Bill Sharp,
Effective Images.
❖❖❖◆❖❖

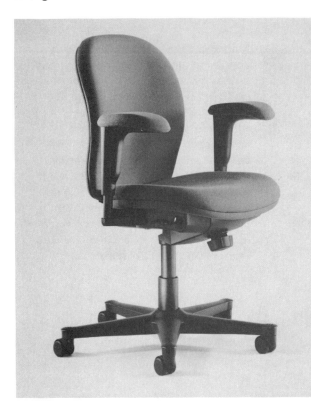

Figure 8-5
Herman Miller's Ambi Chair offers high-value seating, designed to fit both user and task. Its name is derived from the Latin word for "both"; the chair's adaptability allows it to perform as either a general office chair or a dedicated task chair. It fits both large and small people, from the 5th percentile for women, to the 95th percentile for men. Arms adjust for height, and pivot inward or outward for keyboarding adjustment. Highly advanced synchronous tilt mechanism, standard pneumatic height adjustment, and adjustable back height are featured, along with a variety of optional adjustments. Meets ANSI-HFES VDT-Workstation standard.
Courtesy of Herman Miller for the Home, Zeeland, MI. Photo by Nick Merrick, © Hedrich-Blessing.
✧✧◆✧✧

Figure 8-6
The Knoll group's SoHo Chair is an excellent task seating choice for home office workers who want ergonomic support and high design at an affordable price. This chair has a distinctive contemporary look, and sophisticated comfort features, such as a unique sliding seat with synchronized back tilt, pneumatic seat height adjustment, and tension tilt and tilt lock adjustments. It meets BIFMA requirements for durability and OSHA standards for ergonomic comfort. It comes in five upholstery colors and with a five-year warranty.
Courtesy of The Knoll Group, New York, NY.
✧✧◆✧✧

Figure 8-7
Haworth's Improv desk chair was designed to provide maximum comfort and ergonomic support for users whose job functions involve moderately repetitive work. Design direction centered on issues of user comfort, environmental concern, and price minimization. High- and mid-back models are available; pneumatic height adjustment, synchronized tilt, with tension control and back lock are standard. Molded seat and back cushions, enhanced lumbar design, task-supportive seat angle, and a "waterfall" seat pan edge are also featured. The chair meets ANSI and BIFMA standards.
Courtesy of Haworth, Inc., Holland, MI.
✧✧◆✧✧

Figure 8-8
This managerial mid-back chair from the Durable series, by LA Z BOY, features molded arms that resist cuts and scratches.
Courtesy of LA Z Boy Business Furniture, Monroe, MI.
✧◆✧✧✧

Figure 8-9
Global's Operator's chair has the following adjustments: pneumatic seat height, back height, seat angle, back angle, arm height. In addition it is equipped with Air Support[TM] *—lean forward, and the back support system will automatically fill with air. To decrease support, press the air valve while leaning back into the chair.*
Courtesy of Global Industries Inc., Marlton, NJ.
❖❖◆❖❖

Figure 8-10
Another view of a Global Operator's chair.
Courtesy of Global Industries Inc., Marlton, NJ.

Figure 8-11
Global's Anxis series has a sleek shell design and integrated contoured arms. Shown here is the low back model. Molded foam cushions provide long wear. The following adjustments are available: tilt tension and tilt lock; pneumatic seat height; and knee-tilt, which allows you to recline with greater ease while allowing feet to remain comfortably on the floor.
Courtesy of Global Industries Inc., Marlton, NJ.

Figure 8-12
Global's Centra series has laminated
wood arms and a wood capped steel
base. The high-back version is shown,
although you can also get a low-back,
and a matching pull-up sled base. The
chair has a knee-tilt mechanism.
Courtesy of Global Industries Inc., Marlton, NJ.
✧✧✧◆✧✧

Figure 8-13
For those who prefer a fully
upholstered closed arm chair, Global
offers their Halina series. Shown is the
low-back tilter. A sled base guest
armchair is also available.
Courtesy of Global Industries Inc., Marlton, NJ.
✧✧◆✧✧✧

Figure 8-14
The high-back tilter from the Global Halina series.

Courtesy of Global Industries Inc., Marlton, NJ.
❖❖◆❖❖

Figure 8-15
Open-arm chair for Global's Monogram Series. These wood-trimmed, upholstered guest armchairs are appropriate for pull-ups, waiting, or conferencing.

Courtesy of Global Industries Inc., Marlton, NJ.
❖❖❖◆❖❖

Figure 8-16
**The closed-arm version
of Global's Monogram
series.**
Courtesy of Global Industries Inc.,
Marlton, NJ.
✧✧✧◆✧✧

Figure 8-17
**Global's Key series
stacking chairs, chrome
frame with upholstered
seat and back, are also
available in an arm
version.**
Courtesy of Global Industries Inc.,
Marlton, NJ.
◆✧✧✧✧

Figure 8-18
This tub-style chair can be used as a side chair, or if ordered with casters, as pull-up seating. Majic Series.
Courtesy of Global Industries Inc., Marlton, NJ.
✧✧◆✧✧

Figure 8-19
A leather high-back multitilter, from Global's Optima series. Notice the five-star base, which is an important safety feature.
Courtesy of Global Industries Inc., Marlton, NJ.
✧✧✧◆✧✧

Figure 8-20
A managerial chair from the Orians collection by LA Z BOY. It may be ordered in a variety of fabrics; seat and back cushions are designed for easy removal, so you can update fabrics without replacing the entire chair.
Courtesy of LA Z Boy Business Furniture, Monroe, MI.
◇◇◇◆◇◇

Figure 8-21
Global's Planner series drafting chair. Here is a drafting/ graphic artist's chair with a posture back style, where the back angle is controlled by a single lever. A chrome footrest and pneumatic seat height adjustments are standard. This model is also available with comfortable urethane loop-type arms.
Courtesy of Global Industries, Inc., Marlton, NJ.
◇◇◆◇◇◇

Figure 8-22
This very attractive mobile stool has an adjustable seat height, a soft seat, a five-star base for safety, and a foot ring.
Courtesy of The Alma Group, Elkhart, IN.
◇◇◆◇◇

Figure 8-23
Alma's Big Chair is one of the very few chairs on the market that is specifically designed for large individuals.
Courtesy of The Alma Group, Elkhart, IN
◇◇◇◆◇◇

Figure 8-24
The brainchild of a physical therapist, and
former rehabilitation specialist at the
Mayo Clinic, the ZackBack® Computer
Chair is designed to stabilize the spine
through multiadjustable supports that are
individually fitted above and below the
lumbar spine (lower back). It prevents the
individual from assuming a slumped seating
posture. When adjusted for an individual
with neck or back pain, the results are
often dramatic. It features pneumatic
seat-height adjustment and adjustable
armrests.

Courtesy of ZackBack® International, Inc., Rochester, MN.
✧✧✧◆✧✧

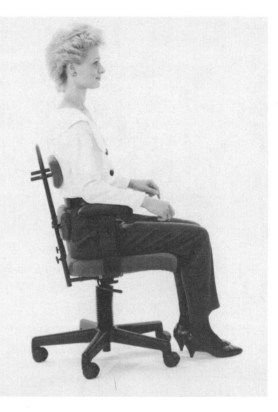

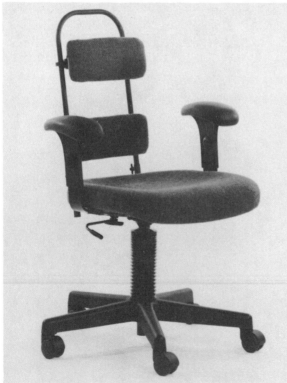

Figure 8-25
Another view of the ZackBack® chair.
Courtesy of ZackBack® International, Inc., Rochester, MN.

Figure 8-26
Aeron chair by Herman Miller, the next generation of work chairs. The distinctive appearance of the Aeron chair is an expression of its unique capabilities and innovative materials. The breakthrough features are too many to mention, the chair offers true cross-performance capability—the first successful union of management, task, conference, and lounge seating. Different sized chairs are available to accommodate user diversity, and adjustments within each chair allow for the same.
Courtesy of Herman Miller Inc., Zeeland, MI. Photo by Nick Merrick © Hedrick-Blessing.
✧✧✧✧◆✧

CHAPTER NINE
ORGANIZING FILING AND STORAGE

Buro 3000 environment.
Courtesy of 3K Möbel, Irvine, CA.

THE WAY YOU SET UP STORAGE for your home office depends on the work you do, your personal preferences, and the space you have available.

Standard Document Sizes

In a typical office, the form that most documents take will be $8\frac{1}{2} \times 11$ inch sheets of paper. Another name for this standard American format is "A" size. Most administrative documents, such as invoices, bills, correspondence, and so on, are of the "A" format.

One or more sheets of paper dealing with a single topic, category, or client are typically grouped in a manila file folder; file folders can then be arranged together in larger file folders.

In most offices project documents are usually "A" size too, although legal documents are $8\frac{1}{2} \times 14$ inches, and accounting spreadsheets can be of varying sizes, up to $8\frac{1}{2} \times 17$ inches, which is called the "B" size format.

Special Project Documents

Drawings, maps, photographic archives, and other specialized documents can be of varied sizes and will require special filing methods. A number of storage units are made for large format, or nonstandard documents. They are often sold through stores that specialize in providing products to a particular industry.

Active Storage Organization

Active storage should be organized and accessible to your workstations for on-call immediate use. The goal is to quickly identify, retrieve, and replace documents to their storage locations.

Documents

Most people elect to put document groups into manila file folders, which can be labeled on the protruding marking tab. In turn, these files can be put into "accordion files" to be maintained as a group on a shelf, or they can be hung in suspension files in a drawer.

Desks usually have file drawers below the work surface, which can be set up for either letter ($8\frac{1}{2} \times 11$) or legal ($8\frac{1}{2} \times 14$) size files. In these file drawers, you can store by "suspension," or by using accordion folders to hold file folders in subgroups. If the file drawer is not equipped for suspension, you can purchase an insert from which you can suspend files.

The pros and cons of the two systems are discussed later in this chapter.

Supplies

In addition to file drawers, workstation furniture may have pencil drawers (usually about 1 inch deep), and/or box drawers (usually between 4 and 6 inches deep). Pencil drawers are good for storing small, flat tools; box drawers are good for keeping larger hand tools and supplies off the work surface when not in use. It is usually convenient to have a box drawer to the right or left of your sitting area, so that you can store frequently used items such as pens, erasers, postage, rubber stamps, checkbook, rubber bands, and the like. If you have to get up from your main work surface for any of these things, your efficiency will be eroded. If you leave them on the desk surface, you will clutter it.

Drawer space is something to keep in mind when you shop for workstation furniture. If you "build" a workstation using a flat top and rectangular support pedestals, you will find that there are a variety of drawer configurations available.

Drawer Storage Independent of Workstations

Aside from pedestal storage, there are a variety of freestanding drawer storage units that you can purchase, in wood or metal. The two basic formats are lateral and vertical.

Vertical file units are deeper than they are wide. They are mostly a minimum of 24 inches from a wall, and some are as deep as 30 inches.

So many of these have been manufactured over the years, that they are readily available from used furniture dealers. Quite often they are resprayed to look almost new.

Lateral file units have a shallower profile, and their drawers are wider than they are deep. Files are typically stored from left to right, rather than front to back.

Both vertical and lateral file units can be purchased with as many as five drawers stacked above each other. In the latter style, the higher drawers usually have "flipper" doors on the face; the exposed opening may roll out for access to files, or it may simply be used for supplies. Lateral file units with flipper doors may be used in lieu of open shelving. With the doors closed you maintain a higher degree of privacy and security. You also hide the visual clutter, and you maintain a clean, linear look. This kind of storage may be very useful in a shared space, such as a family room or den, or in any room where appearance is important.

Accordion versus Suspension Filing

As discussed previously, there are two ways to store files in a file drawer. One way is to tuck documents inside a manila file, and to put the file in an open-topped accordion file. You can get accordion files in varying expansion sizes, depending on how many subfiles you will have inside. The nice part about this storage system is that you can conveniently take the whole file out when you are working on it. The job file then becomes transportable, or relocatable, as a unit. The accordion file can also be stored on a shelf, or easily placed in an "inactive file" cardboard storage box.

Another way to store files in a drawer is to "suspend" the manila file in a hanging file folder. These suspension folders have metal tips on the end and are designed to hang individually from top-mounted rods in the drawers, or from inserts that are fitted into the drawers.

The advantage of this system is that you can glide each file along the suspension hanger, which allows you free and easy access to pull manila files out of the hanging file folder. There are also some disadvantages to this system: (1) the hanging file folders are somewhat costly, although entirely reusable; (2) they take up room—up to half the available storage space in a drawer can be taken up by the hanging file folders, thereby reducing the actual record storage available in the drawer; and (3) if you put a very large file in a hanging file folder, it will sometimes sag and curl from its own weight.

I use both systems in my home office. Projects get accordion files; as the project grows, I enlarge the accordion file or add new ones. Administrative records get hanging files. That seems to work best for me. You may wish to do your own experimenting.

Drawer Unit Quality

There is a broad range of quality in drawer units; if you buy at the bottom end, you are wasting your money. I recommend a full extension drawer on glides with ball-bearing rollers. Before you buy a unit, you may want to test a drawer by fully loading it, and testing its operation. A good file drawer, when weighted down heavily, will continue to open smoothly. Also, when the drawer is open, you shouldn't be able to twist the face easily (an indicator of how sturdily the unit is constructed).

Drawers and Safety

Drawer files, especially lateral files, can tip over on a user, if loaded improperly, or if they do not have built-in tip resistance mechanisms. This situation has resulted in numerous injuries, and in rare but notable cases, injuries have been fatal. You want to be especially cautious when you introduce lateral files into a home environment, where children and pets roam freely.

Some file units have internal latching mechanisms that prevent a user from opening more than one drawer at a time. That keeps the weight in balance, reducing the possibility of tipping. Several manufacturers now provide lead weights, tucked into the back of the unit as a counterbalance.

You can reduce the chance of injury by loading the bottom drawers first. The best safety measure is to fasten the unit to a wall, through the back of the unit, at the level of the highest drawer.

Metal Shelving

One of the least expensive ways to organize storage is with open metal shelving, security and aesthetic issues notwithstanding.

Metal shelving can be of the industrial type, which is almost always purchased ready-to-assemble. Typically a unit consists of gray corner posts with gray metal shelves that are assembled with bolts and nuts supplied. This type of shelving may also be found in black or white, and some manufacturers may even offer a pastel color or two.

There is a broad spectrum of quality in metal shelving. You can purchase light-gauge RTA shelving units in just about any discount department store. For heavier gauges, you may have to go to an office supply or industrial supply company.

Metal shelving can also be purchased preassembled. These units usually have five enclosed sides, and the shelves are adjustable. They are visually more appealing, and they offer a little more protection for stored items. Cost is considerably more than for RTA industrial-style shelving.

Books, especially directories, put a very heavy load on shelving. Tightly packed files will also weigh down a shelf.

Light-gauge metal shelving can crimp under the weight of heavy paper or book storage. Be certain that the shelving you buy will support the loads you intend to put on it.

Wood Shelving Wood shelf units can be purchased preassembled, or RTA. They fall into two categories: particleboard and hardwood.

Wood units can provide a warmer, more homey feeling to an office than comparable metal units.

The panels in particleboard units are faced with a variety of finish coverings, including plastic laminate, as well as wood veneer. It is sometimes hard to tell the difference between a veneered particleboard unit and a solid wood unit.

Probably the greatest difference between a particleboard shelf and a hardwood shelf is strength. A solid wood shelf of the same dimensions will deform (sag) less than one of particleboard. A manufacturer can compensate for this by strengthening the edges of the particleboard, although this adds cost to the unit. The free length of a shelf will also affect its strength. Be particularly careful about lengths over 30 inches.

Desktop Organizers Manufacturers have developed some "cool" desktop organizational systems for files, day-to-day supplies, small work tools, and even desktop electronic equipment. We've included some of these new products at the end of this chapter.

Inactive Storage Documents, supplies and equipment that you don't need to access regularly can be stored in a location remote from your immediate work space. You may want to split locations for document, supply, and equipment storage, for space or security reasons.

Security Documents and equipment are a generally higher security priority than office supplies. Documents may be irreplaceable; equipment usually has higher replacement cost than supplies.

Documents should be stored in such a way as to minimize the possibility of damage by fire and water, as well as animal damage. Be sure that everything is stored off the floor in potentially wet areas. If your storage is subject to damage by moisture, you may want to consider purchasing a dehumidifier, or storing the most perishable documents in a less vulnerable location.

Some equipment is sensitive to moisture and temperature variations. Equipment is more sensitive to theft than documents or supplies, because it can be resold.

You may want to keep your equipment in a locked metal cabinet, and in a storage location that is less vulnerable to intrusion.

Organization If you are storing legal or letter size documents, I recommend that you purchase standard-size storage boxes from an office supply company. They are relatively inexpensive, and they are made for storing documents. They are strong and stackable; they come with covers that will protect your documents; they have a location for labeling contents; and most important, they are all the same size. Standardization of your storage container sizes will dramatically simplify organization and retrieval.

An enhancement to boxed document storage is to put the boxes on open metal shelving. I use 36-inch-wide, light-gauge units that I purchased at a local outlet. They are 12 inches deep, so I let the storage boxes overhang by about 4 inches. I put two boxes onto a shelf. This system helps me in two ways. First, it keeps the boxes off the floor. Second, when I want to retrieve a document, I don't have to unpile a stack of boxes to get into the bottom one. Every box has the label visible, and every box can be pulled independently from the shelving.

There are now a variety of containers on the market that will help you to store your documents and supplies neatly and efficiently. This chapter includes some of these products; you can obtain catalogs by contacting companies listed in the Directory of Contributors.

Storage and Insurance As we have seen, there are several ways to store documents, and some ways are more secure than others. As security increases, the cost of the storage systems increases. Open shelf storage, which is probably the least expensive way to go, provides the least security, because it is especially vulnerable to fire and water damage. Closed storage, which involves a cabinet that is encased on all sides, will provide better protection, but will not ordinarily be fire resistant.

File cabinets that are built to resist fire are very heavy, and the number of shapes and sizes available are limited. Additionally, fire-resistant cabinets can be very expensive.

Although they certainly offer considerably more security than standard cabinets, no system is completely fireproof.

If your documents are irreplaceable, or if you plan to obtain document insurance, fire-resistant cabinets may be necessary. In the application process, document insurers will want to know what kinds of cabinets you use, and they may refuse to write a policy unless you comply with their standards.

Cost Range Code

Below each caption you will notice a horizontal group of diamonds, one of which is blackened. As the blackened diamond moves from left to right, comparative costs rise. *This is a cost-range code only, and its purpose is to give you a general sense of price* relative to similar products or manufacturers. Notice that there is no specific price attached to any of the diamonds or ranges. Prices will vary based on configurations and finishes chosen. Also, dealer pricing varies widely and changes regularly. You can, however, obtain specific pricing on any item shown in this book by calling the phone numbers listed for each provider in the Directory of Contributors.

Figure 9-1
Two of HON's pedestal file units, excellent for supporting work surface tablets, for the do-it-yourself workstation maker. Finished top allows you to use it independently, as a phone or accessory stand. Continuous recessed pulls provide neat appearance, and less chance of scrapes. Shown are pencil-box–file arrangement and double file drawer unit.
Courtesy of the HON Company, Muscatine, IA.
◇◇◆◇◇

Figure 9-2
These units are referred to as vertical files. Shown are pedestals and four-drawer units in legal and letter size widths to suit your filing requirements, whatever they are. HON, a standard for the industry, makes a sturdy unit, with good quality extension glides and hardware. Higher drawers are harder to access, especially the rear files. Also, verticals protrude farther from the walls than laterals (see lateral files below).

Courtesy of the HON Company, Muscatine, IA.
✧✧✦✧✧

Figure 9-3
Lateral files offer shallower depth against walls, conserving on floor space, and allowing easier access to records. When the drawer is extended, you have open view of and access to of all records from left to right. Shown here in a variety of widths and heights.

Courtesy of the HON Company, Muscatine, IA.
✧✧✧✦✧✧

Figure 9-4
These laterals have continuous pulls; grouped together, the drawers call less attention to themselves, and a provide clean linear visual appearance.

Courtesy of Global Industries, Inc., Marlton, NJ.
❖❖❖◆❖❖

Figure 9-5
3K Möbel Manager series. This proportionally handsome RTA component system from 3K Möbel shows its versatility. The variety of doors, drawers, and shelves available give you a chance to design your own storage unit.

Courtesy of 3K Möbel, Irvine, CA.
❖❖❖◆❖❖

Figure 9-6
Warm wood folding bookcase ships and stores
flat, then pops open ready for use right out of
the box.

Courtesy of Hold Everything, San Francisco, CA.
✧◆✧✧✧

Figure 9-7
Versatile shelving in
Herman Miller's JB system
allows you to neatly store
a variety of different-sized
items, keep them dust-
free and out-of-sight
behind closed doors. (See
pages 101 and 102 for
another view of this
system.)

Courtesy of Herman Miller for the
Home, Zeeland, MI. Photo by
Nick Merrick, © Hedrich-Blessing.
✧✧✧◆✧✧

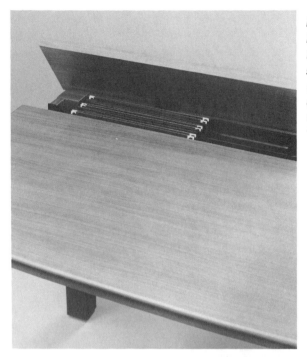

Figure 9-8
Flipper door at the rear of Turnstone's Docker desk reveals space for filing, small work tools, and wire management. (See pages 99 and 100 for views of the complete desk and system.)
Courtesy of Steelcase, Inc., Grand Rapids, MI.
◇◇◇◆◇◇

Figure 9-9
Detail of O'Sullivan's Scandinavian collection, showing suspension filing system supported by wood sides of drawers; note extension glides on drawers. (See page 85 for a view of the system.)
Courtesy of O'Sullivan Industries, Lamar, MO.
◇◇◆◇◇◇

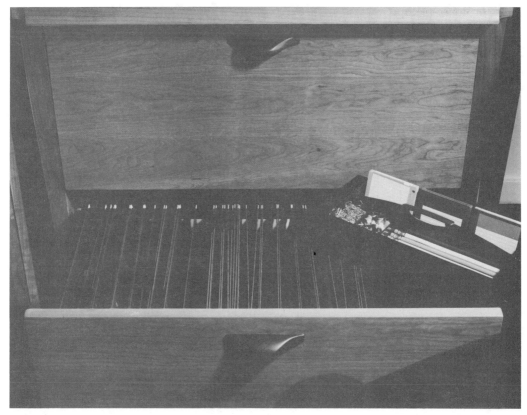

Figure 9-10
Detail of lateral file component, Herman Miller's TD system. Included is a small work tool tray,
which sits on the suspension rack of the file drawer.
Courtesy of Herman Miller for the Home, Zeeland, MI. Photo by Eliot Kaufman Photography.
✧✧✧✧♦✧

Figure 9-11
Rolling file caddies be
tucked out of way when
not in use, rolled into
position when needed, or
to another station.
Courtesy of Hold Everything, San
Francisco, CA.
✧♦✧✧✧

Figure 9-12
Container Store's®
wire roll-around unit,
matches to their
do-it-yourself
workstation system
(see pages 79 and 80).
Courtesy of The Container
Store®, Dallas, TX.
✧◆✧✧✧

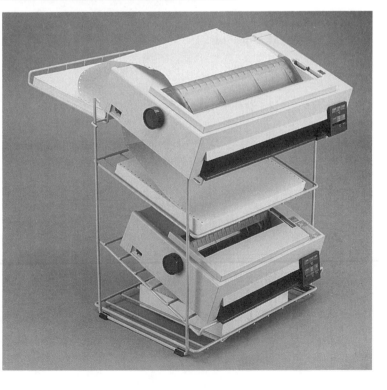

Figure 9-13
This unit by Balt
organizes two printers
and paper on one stand,
for dual printing desktop
applications. Balt offers a
stacking unit for just
about any configuration.
Courtesy of Balt, Inc., Cameron, TX.
✧◆✧✧✧

Figure 9-14
Balt's low profile utility stand has a collection basket, and a storage shelf below. Made of powder-coated steel. Casters shown are optional.
Courtesy of Balt, Inc., Cameron, TX.
✧◆✧✧✧

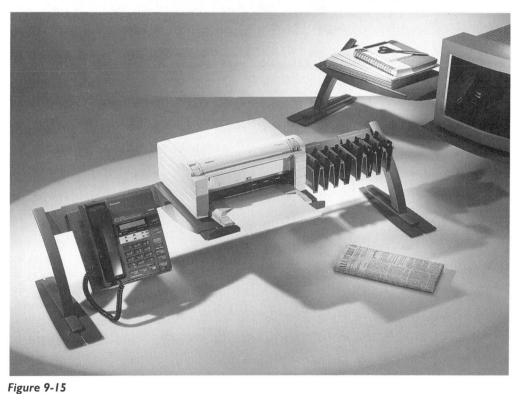

Figure 9-15
Details' free-standing WorkFlo rail allows you to position a variety of support elements along a horizontal member. Elevated rail keeps the work surface open. Shown here are the diskette/note holder, telephone caddie, and equipment supports that hold up to 60 pounds.
Courtesy of Details, Inc., New York, NY.
✧✧✧◆✧✧

Figure 9-16
Similar to the freestanding unit, this WorkFlo rail is panel-mounted, freeing the work surface completely. Notice the variety of support and storage elements available.
Courtesy of Details, Inc., New York, NY.
✧✧◆✧✧

Figure 9-17
This is a wall-mounted application of SlatWall, which can be mounted onto panels or drywall. Support tools shown are tack strip, pencil cup, telephone caddie, binder holder, and a side access folder. Use your wall, and keep your work surface free for projects.
Courtesy of Details, Inc., New York, NY.
✧✧✧◆✧✧

CHAPTER TEN
ERGONOMIC TOOLS

Understanding that home computer users need the same ergonomic support as office workers, Knoll developed the Surf line as three freestanding pieces—wrist wrest, mouse pad, and footrest—which help to alleviate strain and discomfort of extended computer use.
Courtesy of The Knoll Group, New York, NY.

A S YOU KNOW BY NOW, AN AMAZING VARIETY of home office products have been recently introduced into the marketplace. This is also certainly true of ergonomic equipment for the home office, especially as it relates to workstations.

If you are purchasing new workstation furniture, you may find that several ergonomic features are already "built in" to your new unit, especially for computer use. There are also many add-on products that will modify a station for wrist and arm support, keyboard flexibility, monitor height and tilt adjustment, mouse use, and so on (see also, Chapter 6, Ergonomics).

Product Features and Benefits

Along with photographs, we have included some descriptive information about the products, mainly, but not exclusively, from information the manufacturer provided. Warranties of function, quality and performance will be only those offered by the manufacturer at time of purchase.

Trial Periods

There is no such thing as a product that solves all problems, or works for everyone. Furthermore, you may be purchasing these items through a mail order company. That's why it is important to be able to use these items for a brief trial period, and to return them if necessary. Reputable companies will allow you to return items, minus modest shipping and restocking fees. Be sure that you are allowed this latitude as a condition of purchase.

Cost Range Code

Below each caption you will notice a horizontal group of diamonds, one of which is blackened. As the blackened diamond moves from left to right, comparative costs rise. *This is a cost-range code only, and its purpose is to give you a general sense of price* relative to similar products or manufacturers. Notice that there is no specific price attached to any of the diamonds or ranges. Prices will vary based on configurations and finishes chosen. Also, dealer pricing varies widely and changes regularly. You can, however, obtain specific pricing on any item shown in this book by calling the phone numbers listed for each provider in the Directory of Contributors.

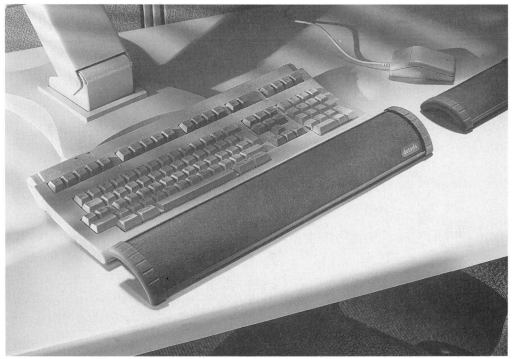

Figure 10-1
Recurve™ Palm Rest, designed for rest in between keying. Freestanding, height adjustable, for positive or negative tilt.
Courtesy of Details, Inc., New York, NY.
❖❖◆❖❖

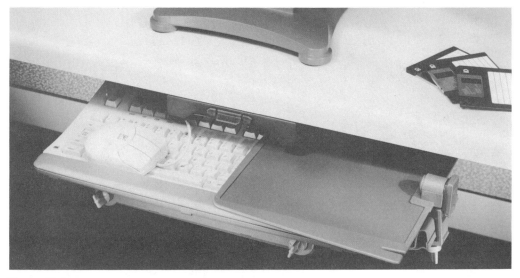

Figure 10-2
Details' keyboard holder raises, lowers, swivels, and tilts to maximize keying comfort throughout the day. It attaches to underside of any work surface over 20 inches deep. Cushioned palm rest is height adjustable. Mouse tray folds over and out of the way.
Courtesy of Details, Inc., New York, NY.
❖❖◆❖❖

Figure 10-3
Another view of the Details keyboard holder with the mouse tray deployed.
Courtesy of Details, Inc., New York, NY.

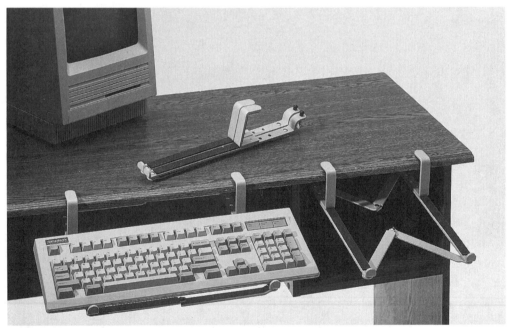

Figure 10-4
Portable keyboard holder and mouse support assembly, can be attached to work surfaces of varying thicknesses, up to 2.5 inches, and can be easily removed and relocated. Contact points are rubber cushioned and the unit folds flat for easy storage.
Courtesy of Balt, Inc., Cameron, TX.
✧◆✧✧✧✧

Figure 10-5
The Kinesis ® Ergonomic Keyboard is shaped and contoured to conform to keying movements of the fingers and hands, limiting force and physical stress. PC compatible and Mac compatible with optional interface box.
© Kinesis ® Corporation, Bothell, WA.
✧✧✦✧✧

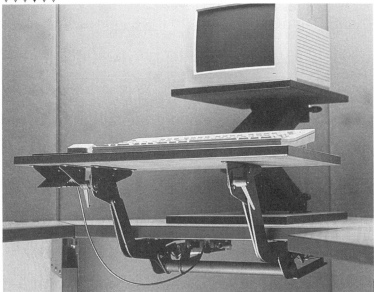

Figure 10-6
Adjusta Surface may be positioned for seating or standing positions, from the tallest to shortest user and from wheelchair to task chair position. Spring assisted counterbalanced mechanism eliminates cranking and allows adjustments to be made quickly and easily with minimum effort.
Courtesy of Flex-Y-Plan Industries, Inc., Fairview, PA.
✧✧✦✧✧

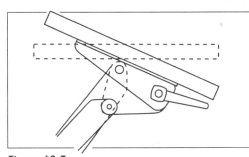

Figure 10-7
Range of Adjusta Surface's tilting positions.
Courtesy of Flex-Y-Plan Industries, Inc., Fairview, PA.

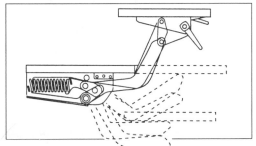

Figure 10-8
View of Adjusta Surface's spring mechanism.
Courtesy of Flex-Y-Plan Industries, Inc., Fairview, PA.

Figure 10-9
Elegant Monitor Lift
may be positioned
vertically with
minimum effort.

Courtesy of Details, Inc.,
New York, NY.
❖❖❖◆❖❖

Figure 10-10
Monitor Lift in another
position.

Courtesy of Details, Inc.,
New York, NY.

Figure 10-11
Monitor blocks come in packs of three and are stackable as shown. They raise the monitor and provide storage space all in one, integrated wire management is located at back.
Courtesy of Details, Inc., New York, NY.
✧✦✧✧✧✧

Figure 10-12
Closeup rear view of Monitor blocks' wire management.
Courtesy of Details, Inc., New York, NY.

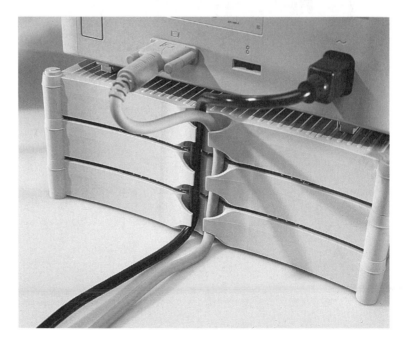

Figure 10-13
Ergonomic Logic specializes in providing products that transform your existing, nonadjustable workstation into a completely adjustable working environment. Shown here monitor riser, footrest, Ergorest™ articulating arm support, with integrated mouse pad, and task chair.
Courtesy of Ergonomic Logic, Inc., Sparks, NV.
✧✧✦✧✧

Figure 10-14
Details' footrest has four height adjustments from 2 to 6 inches.
Courtesy of Details, Inc., New York, NY.
✧✧◆✧✧

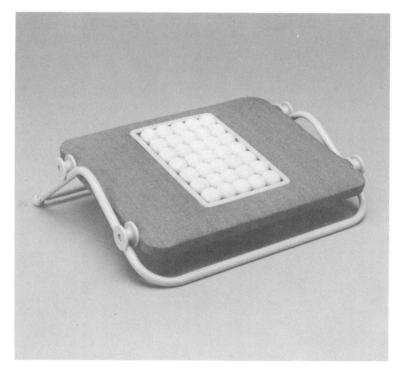

Figure 10-15
Rolax™ adjustable footrest has multipositioning for optimum relief of foot and back fatigue. Plush, padded, comfortable surfaces surround natural wood roller balls, which massage feet and reduce leg pressure.
Courtesy of Balt, Inc., Cameron, TX.
✧✧◆✧✧

CHAPTER ELEVEN

TASK LIGHTING

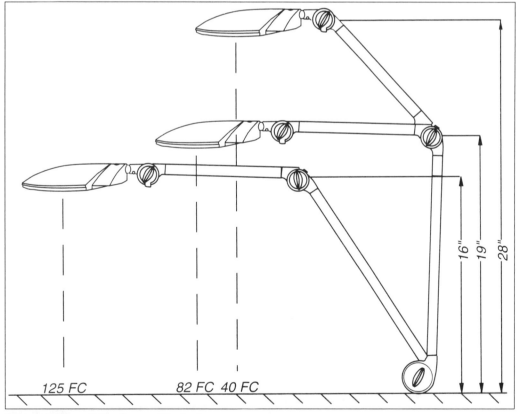

Courtesy of Waldmann Lighting Company, Wheeling, IL.

EVEN IF NATURAL LIGHT STREAMS into your home office, there are a number of reasons to introduce artificial light. First of all, light varies depending upon weather, time of day, and time of year. Second, there may be times when you need to shade natural light because of glare or heat gain.

Task Lighting Explained

Most people are familiar with the typical recessed fluorescent fixtures in the hung ceilings of typical office space. This type of light is called *ambient light*. It spreads itself all around, hence the name. The other type of light is *task light*, which focuses on a very specific, or task, area.

A gooseneck lamp is a kind of task light, although task lighting can also emanate from the ceiling (surface mounted or recessed spotlights). Some lamps, such as a desk lamp with a translucent shade, provide task and ambient lighting simultaneously.

It is usually best to have a combination of task and ambient lighting in your office space. Sharp contrasts of light and dark within a space can be a strain on the eyes. If you are working in a room with no ceiling lighting, you might want to think about purchasing a torchière, which is a floor lamp designed to light your ceiling, which in turn provides some ambient light in your office.

Light Source as a Problem Source

The selection and arrangement of the proper lighting in an office requires careful thinking. Inappropriate choices of lighting may produce unwanted reflections on computer screens, direct glare, or inadequate amounts of coverage or brightness on work surfaces.

Lighting also generates heat; the selection and placement of light must also be considered, along with the ventilating and air conditioning issues in a space.

Halogen and Fluorescent Sources

The old fashioned "A-lamp" or tungsten filament bulb is rapidly being replaced by new light sources, such as miniaturized fluorescent tubes and halogen sources. These light sources can't be simply put into old lamps that used tungsten bulbs, because the power they require needs transformation. This is accomplished somewhere within the lamp fixture.

Halogen sources have some interesting advantages. They generate a lot of light from a relatively small point source, which allows the fixture designers to make very small, almost transparent units. Halogen devotees also like the color balance of halogen, which more closely resembles the spectrum of natural sunlight. Halogen lamps often come with built-in dimmers.

The miniaturized fluorescent sources have larger heads, but their sources remain comparatively cool. Another benefit of fluorescent light is that it disperses more uniformly over a surface area. In terms of color cast, fluorescent light isn't as "warm" as either tungsten or halogen.

Glare   Glare can come from two sources: either directly from the light source (the "bulb") or from a reflected source.

Some manufacturers take great pains to reduce direct glare, by designing the head of the lamp with a baffling unit, which is sometimes referred to as an egg crate, because of its many rectangular slots.

Another way to reduce direct glare is either by positioning the lamp head behind you, or by moving it below eye level. In either case light can't be directly transmitted into your eye. The problem with putting the source behind you is that your body may throw an unwanted shadow on a portion of the work surface area.

Since you will most likely be positioning the lamp you use on the desk in front of you, a lamp with a movable head will help you control glare.

Flexible Arm   If you have lots of space on your work surface, but your area
Task Lights   of work concentration is confined, you may want to choose something that sits right on the work surface, the typical lamp with a base.

If your work spreads out over a large surface area, you may want to purchase a lamp with a flexible arm, and one that is clamped to the edge of the work surface, so that it doesn't take up valuable desk space. Some manufacturers offer a choice of base or clamp for the same fixture, so that you can choose the best arrangement for your needs.

Another benefit to a flexible arm task light is that you can lower it to concentrate light over a specific part of your work surface, or move it high at other times to illuminate a broader surface area.

A flexible arm also gives you the opportunity to control screen glare, by lowering or tilting the head of the task light so that light doesn't reflect back into your eyes.

Dimmers   A task light with a built-in dimmer will allow you to control brightness from the source, which can come in very handy when you are working at a computer. If you are using a tungsten (standard bulb) lamp, you can purchase a dimmer separately, with which you may reduce the amount of power going to the source, thereby dimming it. Many halogen products have dimmers already included within the fixture. Fluorescent dimming is a complicated process, but in general, compact fluorescent sources emit less glare than their halogen or tungsten counterparts.

Try It First   The only way to be sure that a task light will work properly for you is to try it out for a few days. When you purchase, be certain that you will be able to have a reasonable trial period, so that you may test the unit under actual working conditions.

Cost Range   Below each caption you will notice a horizontal group of
Code   diamonds, one of which is blackened. As the blackened diamond moves from left to right, comparative costs rise. *This is a cost-range code only, and its purpose is to give you a general sense of price* relative to similar products or manufacturers. Notice that there is no specific price attached to any of the diamonds or ranges. Prices will vary based on configurations and finishes chosen. Also, dealer pricing varies widely and changes regularly. You can, however, obtain specific pricing on any item shown in this book by calling the phone numbers listed for each provider in the Directory of Contributors.

Figure 11-1
IOS task light has an articulating arm for flexibility, and a compact fluorescent lamp source at its head, which provides cool, widespread light with little glare. Available in panel-mount or freestanding base mount version, shown.

Courtesy of Details, Inc., New York, NY.
✧✧◆✧✧

Figure 11-2
A parabolic louver at the source also helps to disperse light and prevent direct glare when the head of the lamp is above eye level. Shown here is a Valencia ergonomic task light, which also is equipped with two 9-watt compact fluorescent lamps, which produce the same light as a 75-watt incandescent lamp, but utilize 77% less energy produce less and heat.

Courtesy of Waldmann Lighting Company, Wheeling, IL.
✧✧✧◆✧✧

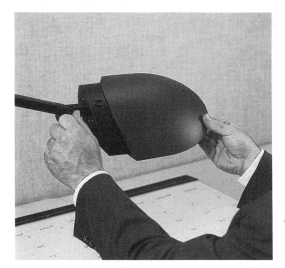

Figure 11-3
A good task lamp should have flexible movement, both in the arm and at the head.
Courtesy of Waldmann Lighting Company, Wheeling, IL.

Figure 11-4
Waldmann's Valencia series allows you to choose from four mounting bases: table base, panel bracket, wall bracket, and clamp.
Courtesy of Waldmann Lighting Company, Wheeling, IL.
✧✧✧✦✧✧

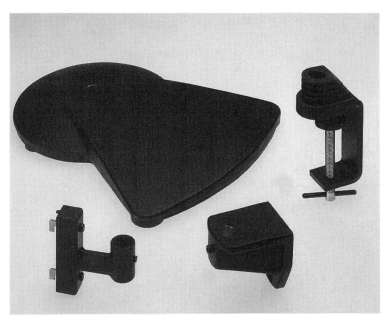

CHAPTER TWELVE
DESKTOP VIDEO

Shown, Live™ PCS 100.
Courtesy of PictureTel Corporation, Danvers, MA.

$\mathbf{O}$NE OF THE MOST EXCITING INNOVATIONS in the world of computers and communications is the advent of inexpensive desktop video. The new teleconferencing equipment that is already being marketed will have an enormous effect on home office and remote office use, because people will be able to connect visually, significantly reducing the feeling of separation and isolation.

The currently developing information superhighway is already providing relatively inexpensive two-way visual communication. As service and equipment costs continue to drop, televisual home offices will soon be as common as car telephones. This will dramatically enhance the quality and the psychological proximity of home-office communication, but it also means that our clients or employers will be able to see us in action. This may mean the end of those occasional sweatsuit workdays, but *hey*, nobody said life's going to be perfect!

"POTS" Video

There are companies who currently manufacture video systems that operate over your existing, plain old telephone system (POTS). The advantage of a POTS video system is that you can use your existing telephone line, thus avoiding additional installation charges as well as monthly and usage charges for a dedicated, or separate, system.

Unfortunately, analog telephone lines can carry only a limited amount of data volume. An analog video system works by taking snapshots and transmitting them to the other end at a much slower rate than what we are accustomed to viewing in normal real-time television. The resulting image is not perfectly fluid; it's more like a series of snapshots, and voice may not be entirely in sync the with image. Another drawback is that each user must currently have an identical terminal system in order to communicate, although a standard for all analog video manufacturers (H 320) will soon be in place. Lastly, this kind of system doesn't transmit data files. Because of these limitations, analog desktop video currently has very limited value for business.

Changes in Business Video Conferencing

Many corporations have had video conference rooms in operation for almost two decades. Service is provided by a dedicated (T-1) line which is installed between two points. For instance, if your company has offices in New York and

San Diego, the phone company sets up a specialized, dedicated line for you between those two points; this line is devoted to video conferencing, and is independent of your telephone service. It's the video equivalent of telegraph's transatlantic cable. The terminal conference rooms are more like miniaturized TV studios—elaborate and very expensive.

The *new* video conferencing infrastructure is a *networked* system, similar to the national and international telephone system. You can call any point from any other point, and have interactive communication. All you have to do is connect into the system. You can also make conference calls. The cost of the video equipment and system connection has dropped to the point where home office workers can consider this technology.

The Interconnecting Service

Right now, the most readily available network is the Integrated System Digital Network (ISDN). ISDN is a "hardwire" network system, similar to your normal telephone service. A separate ISDN digital line is brought to your home or office. This line is different from a normal telephone line in that it can carry more data volume, sort of like a larger pipeline. The ISDN system is a network system provided by a consortium of the "Baby Bells."

Although ISDN is currently the standard for business quality desktop video, it also has a somewhat limited bandwidth, compared with the normal American television standard (NTSC). This result is slower frame refreshment (15 per second as opposed to 30 per second) for ISDN. This makes the video image less fluid than television, but far superior to POTS video.

ISDN is not currently available everywhere, but the local telephone companies are rapidly expanding the service areas. If it is available in your area, there is an installation charge, a monthly service charge, and a use charge.

The ISDN network is developing standards that will make it easier for users to hook into the system, and connect with the computer networks of large companies, as well as single-point users. All the bugs aren't entirely worked out, but world standardization is coming.

Another important feature of the ISDN system is that (with the proper terminal equipment and software) you can

Figure 12-1
The C-Phone® Desktop Video Conferencing System, camera/speaker/microphone,
shown mounted above a user's computer monitor. The system gives you the feeling of a
face-to-face meeting.

Courtesy of Target Technologies, Inc., Wilmington, NC.

Figure 12-2
PictureTel Live™ *PCS 50 screen shot, with data and images shown simultaneously.*
Courtesy of PictureTel Corporation, Danvers, MA.

transmit computer data while you are using the teleconferencing system. It is possible for users in two different locations to both manipulate data on-screen in real time, from the same data file, while also having visual contact with each other.

Your Computer and Desktop Video

The system depends on your computer to do the interconnecting brainwork. Since there are several computer platforms, and computers vary in power—even in the same platform—your system may limit your ability to tie into the network. As computers become more powerful, more standardized, and more friendly to each other, network interconnection will eventually become as simple as plugging in your toaster. Right now, it's a bit more complicated, but it's not rocket science either.

If you are thinking about buying a computer in the near future, it would be wise to find out what kind of desktop video interfacing capabilities are already built into the equipment. Some investigation and educated purchasing now may make the video interface easier later.

Video Equipment for the Desktop System

In addition to the interconnecting service and your computer, you also need a camera, a video card for your computer, a speaker/microphone unit, and some operating software. Your computer and your camera then work together, connected to the ISDN line through a modem-like device.

The camera can sit on top of your monitor, or can be positioned on a desktop tripod, and thus can be aimed at various locations, including presentation walls or table surfaces.

Companies such as Target Technologies and PictureTel provide a variety of packages that will convert your computer to a desktop video station.

Other Network Delivery Systems

There are two other communications groups that are also hard at work to create and maintain a share in the marketplace for the delivery of interactive video service. They are the TV cable companies and the cellular satellite companies.

Cable

While all this is happening, the TV cable service providers are busily restringing their service networks so that they can become interactive. That is to say, the old cable systems were one-way; they delivered images to you. In contrast with the ISDN system, the cable system is based on fiber optic technologies as opposed to copper.

Fiber optic lines can transmit a much broader band of data than copper, which may mean that eventually the fiber optic system may become more attractive as a network of use for some or perhaps all users.

Cable companies are developing an array of interactive services for their systems, such as banking and shopping services, security services, network broadcast interactivity, and so on. Networked desktop video conferencing is only one of many choices that will eventually become available to the customer.

Wave

The ultimate system is wireless. A desktop video network using satellites and antennas, similar to cellular telephone

*Figure 12-3
A C-Phone® desktop
video screen shot,
showing a four-party
conference call (the
viewing party is also on
the screen). Currently
available with affordable
add-on technology for
LAN and WAN networks,
this is also a look into the
future potential of home
office desktop video.*

Courtesy of Target Technologies,
Inc., Wilmington, NC.

systems, is within the realm of feasibility. For remote areas and countries that do not have line infrastructure, this communication method will be the first to take hold. Even in major US cities, the cost of providing service through this technology may eventually become competitive with cable (fiber optic) and copper systems.

Effect of Video on Home Office Organization

The most obvious result will be that people are going to feel "closer" as they communicate in a real-time visual format. They will be able to see each others' expressions and emotions, along with visual presentations, voice, and the written word. The moment you tie into this system, you will have to be more concerned about your personal appearance, as well as the appearance and organization of your office. How and where you set up your camera will affect how you organize your personal space. For instance, if you are going to occasionally transmit wall presentations, then an area of your office has to be set up for that. If all you ever plan to transmit is your head-shot, then the backdrop image will be an important consideration.

Depending on how you work and the image you wish to project, you may want a backdrop of bookshelves, or a simple background screen. I imagine that before too long, some creative software developer will design a "merge program" which cuts your image and pastes it over a variety of still or moving backgrounds.

Inexpensive two-way televisual communication will un-doubtedly accelerate the comfort level and convenience of working at a remote site. It is definitely something to be thinking about now, and planning for soon.

CHAPTER THIRTEEN
RENOVATIONS, ADDITIONS,
AND NEW CONSTRUCTION

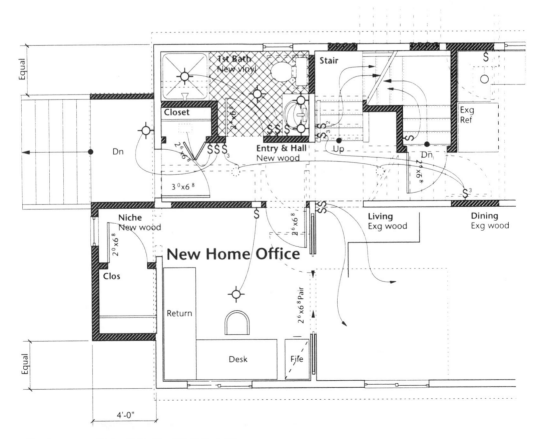

Drawing courtesy of Robert T. Coolidge, AIA, Guilford, CT.

Feasibility If you are considering a renovation or an addition to your home for use as an office, or if you are planning an office within a new home, you should begin with what is commonly called a feasibility study. Don't let the word scare you—all you want to do is see if your intentions make sense. Before you drive the first nail, it is imperative to consider whether your ideas are feasible. Without prior planning, your project could be stopped dead in the middle, for a number of reasons. This preliminary work will help you to:

- describe the size and scope of the project
- understand planning and zoning issues
- evaluate potential construction problems
- estimate project length and cost
- identify potential disruptions due to construction

Size and Scope Before you consider a renovation or addition, you have to determine your specific needs for office space at home (see Chapter 1, Home Office Planning "101"). This first step will help you to determine your basic needs, and how they relate to the rest of your living space. It will also help you to develop a budget for furniture and equipment, which will become part of the overall project budget.

Once you have a sense of size, translated into square feet, and separation, you can realistically analyze your options. We'll talk about the pros and cons of selecting various locations, or "adding-on" later in this chapter.

Planning and Zoning Issues We assume that you are planning to do all renovation and construction with the proper approvals from the local officials. This means that once you have decided what it is that you are going to do, *at a very preliminary stage*, you should definitely check with authorities to see if they will let you do it.

In the case of having an office in the home, it means you must determine that:

- Your town or building association will allow you to run a business out of your house.
- They will allow you to run your type of business.
- The renovations/additions you are proposing will be acceptable to the planning and zoning department, as well as the building (construction) department.

Help from Your Local Authorities

A brief meeting with one of your local town officials will be worth the time and trouble in helping you to understand constraints. Once they know what it is that you are attempting to do, officials can help you to identify limitations before they become catastrophes. They won't be able to help you with cost estimating—that's not their job—but their preliminary review assistance is usually free.

Planning and Zoning Ordinances

Each town has a book or pamphlet outlining rules and regulations governing land usage for the entire town. The book relates to a planning and zoning map that the town has also developed. If you wish, you can purchase the ordinances and map; the town usually has copies you can review for free at the planning and zoning office.

These maps and books can be very confusing to the first-time user (see Figure 13-1). They cross-reference many sections, use their own jargon, and contain several complicated charts and tables. This is where the local planning official can help you. The official can identify the location of your property on the zoning map. If you clearly describe what you wish to do, the official can quickly help you wade through the rules and regulations, focusing in on issues that are important for your specific proposal and can tell you what is or isn't permitted.

Sometimes a use isn't permitted as-of-right, but may be granted by variance. The official can tell you about the process of applying for a variance and give you some idea of how you may fare in the process.

If you are planning to add on to your house, there may be specific requirements for lot coverage and setbacks, which could limit the size and location of your proposed addition.

In this case, you are probably already working with a design professional, who can answer many of these questions.

All this may sound very complicated, but in most cases you will be able to do what you wish, with perhaps some minor limitations or modifications.

Ordinances are distinct from building codes. The ordinances govern usage (see Figure 13-1); the building codes govern construction. In a renovation or addition project, you will ultimately have to comply with both.

Zoning Schedule 1—Use, Area, and Height Controls

District	Principal Uses	Accessory Uses	Special Uses	Type
R-1LL Single family Large lot Residential	Single family detached dwellings Houses of worship	Detached garages Tennis courts Sauna/bathhouses Storage sheds	Private schools Nursing homes Day care centers Bed-and-breakfasts	
R-1A Single family Low density Residential	Single family detached dwellings Houses of worship	Detached garages Tennis courts Sauna/bathhouses Storage sheds	Private schools Nursing homes Day care centers Bed-and-breakfasts	

R-1B
Single family
Medium density
Residential
	Single family
	  detached dwellings
	Houses of worship
		Detached garages
		Tennis courts
		Sauna/bathhouses
		Storage sheds
			Private schools
			Day care centers
			Nursing homes
			Colleges or universities
			  including dormitories
			Bed-and-breakfasts	

R-2A
One- and two-family
Residential
	Single-family
	  and two-family
	  detached dwellings
	Houses of worship
		Detached garages
		Storage sheds
		Home occupations
			Conversions
			Private schools
			Nursing homes
			Day care centers
			Colleges or universities
			  including dormitories
			Bed-and-breakfasts
			Charitable or religious
			  institutions
				One-family
				Two-family

R-2B
One- and two-family
Medium density
Residential
	Single-family
	  and two-family
	  detached dwellings
	Single-family
	  and two-family
	  rowhouses
	Houses of worship
		Detached garages
		Storage sheds
		Home occupations
			Conversions
			Private schools
			Nursing homes
			Day care centers
			Colleges or universities
			  including dormitories
			Bed-and-breakfasts
			Charitable or religious
			  institutions
			Community residences
				Rowhouse
				Detached

R-2C
One- and two-family
Rowhouse
Residential
	Single-family
	  and two-family
	  rowhouses
	Houses of worship
		Detached garages
		Storage sheds
		Home occupations
			Nursing homes
			Charitable or religious
			  institutions
			Day care centers
			Day care homes
			Bed-and-breakfasts
			Community residences
			Adult day care centers
				One-family
				Two-family

R-3A
Multifamily
Low density
Residential
	Single-family
	  and two-family
	  detached dwellings
	Garden apartments
	Houses of worship
		Detached garages
		Storage sheds
		Home occupations
			Community residences
			Private schools
			Nursing homes
			Day care centers
			Charitable or religious
			  institutions
			Colleges or universities
			Bed-and-breakfasts
			Hospitals
				One- and
				  two-family
				Garden
				  apartments

R-3A
Multifamily
Medium density
Residential
	Single-family
	  and two-family
	  detached dwellings
	Single-family
	  and two-family
	  rowhouse dwellings
	Apartment buildings
	Houses of worship
		Detached garages
		Home occupations
		Storage sheds
			All R-3A special uses
			Rooming houses/SROs
				Detached
				One-family
				  rowhouse
				Two-family
				  rowhouse
				Apartments

Figure 13-1
Sample zoning regulation chart.

**Town Ordinances
Specifically
Governing Home
Offices**

If you work alone and clients rarely or never visit you, then most localities will allow you to operate a home office. After all, writers, artists, and salespeople have had a long tradition of working from home. Nevertheless, many towns now require that you obtain a permit to operate a home office. If you intend to have employees and/or clients, your town may be more restrictive.

The decision a town makes about whether to allow you to operate an employee/visitor-based business from your home may be related to the "zone" in which your home is located. Many towns have several residential zones, with varied levels of restriction. Some zones, or streets in certain zones, will allow you to openly conduct professional activities, and display a sign. We see this all the time with doctors, dentists and lawyers. Some zones will not allow this kind of activity at all.

In most towns, there are a number of residential zones, and they may vary with respect to what uses are allowed. This is an especially important consideration if you are planning to buy a house in which you intend to establish a home office.

Town officials can acquaint you with the local ordinances governing home offices. Towns are concerned about traffic, parking, signs, and other things that happen *outside* your home office, as well as the kind of work you do, your employees, and other visitors.

**Condominium
Associations**

The by-laws of condominium associations may be more restrictive than the ordinances of the town in which the condominium is located. Associations will want to review and approve your plans, but their approval does not mean acceptance by the town. In this case, you must obtain planning approval from both the town and the association, as well as building approvals from the town building officials.

Appeals

If you are legally restricted from operating as you wish, you may be able to comply with existing regulations by modifying some aspect of your business operation. Alternatively, you may decide to explain some extenuating circumstance in a formal appeal. In general, towns will not make major exceptions to their zoning ordinances because doing so dilutes the strength of the existing ordinance and sets a precedent that may trigger future disputes. Nevertheless, if you feel that the ordinance is unfairly restrictive, you may wish to consult with a local real estate attorney about your chances of prevailing in an appeal. Many towns are in the process of reevaluating their policy regarding home offices because of the growing number of people who are working at home. A coherently presented appeal may cause them to reconsider and modify policy.

The Building Department
The next step in the preliminary planning process is to meet with an official of your town's building department. A design professional can be your representative, or you can meet with the building department by yourself.

Building officials, who will issue a building permit, inspect construction, and issue a certificate of occupancy, are very interested in knowing what you want to do at the earliest possible time. They don't want to be in the position of requiring you to modify something *after* it has been built.

At this stage, it is extremely helpful to have a rough drawing or plan of your intended building program. There is no need to have a full set of building plans or details —all you are trying to do is get a preliminary "look-see." If there is a problem, your drawings may have to be revised, so the simpler the better.

For example, existing ceiling heights in the basement may not be acceptable for code-compliant living or office space. The existing stair to the attic may not be legal. These are questions that may be raised by the building official.

Variances
If an aspect of your home is noncompliant, the building department may be willing to allow a "variance." If an existing situation doesn't comply with current codes, and would be unfeasible to change, then the building official may offer an alternate solution, or accept the existing condition. These determinations are made on a case-by-case basis, and often require nothing more than filing a one-sheet application for a variance, explaining the circumstances. The building official will give you an opinion about approval.

ADA Requirements
Town building officials may require that you comply with aspects of the Americans with Disabilities Act (ADA), especially if you plan on having visitors or employees.

Preconstruction Analysis

People often have a vision in their minds about how the end product will look and how much they will enjoy their new quarters when complete. They rarely realize how much is involved in the building process, and that, like it or not, they will be in the center of it for weeks, even months. Even if warned explicitly beforehand, they often just don't get the picture.

One thing you can count on is that life is not perfect, and even the "best laid plans" won't be able to take every eventuality into account. Nevertheless, the more thinking and planning you do beforehand, the more knowledgeable assistance you accrue, the easier and smoother the process will be.

If you have never been involved in a serious home construction project, you will probably not be acquainted with the broad range of issues that you will face, or problems that you may encounter. It is impossible for anyone to list every problem or roadblock, much less the proper solution for it when it occurs. That said, I'll try to point out some of the more typical issues, to give you a sense of the variables.

Basements

If you are going to renovate a basement, it is a good idea to build insulated wood-frame walls around the area you will use, including the perimeter foundation. A modest amount of heat supply will then make the space comfortable during the winter months.

The concrete floors of most basements are uninsulated below the concrete. During the winter, the floor can remain cold even though the room temperature is normal. If you are sitting for long periods of time, the floor will absorb heat from your feet, and you can become uncomfortably cold.

This problem can be solved by building an insulated floor above the concrete floor. Carpeting with a good insulating pad below will also help to reduce heat loss.

Basements can become very humid in the warmer months, which can damage paper and equipment, and cause user discomfort. A dehumidifier will solve this problem.

If your basement takes on water, you may want to rethink using the space, unless you can prevent water from entering. There are several methods that can solve this problem, such as sump pumps or foundation treatments. This problem should be solved before considering use as office space, or storage space.

Garages   If you decide to use a garage for office space, you will lose a covered parking space. This may be acceptable to you, but not to the town.

If you are renovating a garage space for office use, you will have insulation and heating concerns as well.

Relocation of Walls   Sometimes interior walls are load-bearing; they are holding up part of the structure above. These walls can be opened, or removed, but not without special construction techniques and introduction of other structural members that will do the work in place of the wall. This is also true if you plan to add a window or door to a load-bearing exterior wall.

If you plan to move or penetrate walls, you may affect the overall building structure, and, unless you are personally familiar with building construction, it would be a good idea to consult a licensed architect or structural engineer before proceeding one step further.

Attics   If you plan to use an attic space or basement space, it is most likely uninsulated.

Attic spaces can be sweltering in warmer months, and frigid in winter months. The introduction of insulation between joists prior to finishing, properly sized and faced, can solve that problem. The new assembly will have to "breathe" properly, or it can damage the structure or roof. You may have to add ridge or soffit ventilation as well.

If you plan on using attic space, you will want to be sure that the structural members (joists) of the existing attic floor are capable of handling live loads. Some attic floors have been designed only to handle light storage and were not intended for use as living space. This can be remedied by additional structural members, but an analysis should be done in the planning stages.

Another problem common to attic space is ceiling clearance. Building codes require certain minimum heights in order for the space to be considered habitable. You can "dormer out" some areas, raising the roof pitch and subsequent ceiling heights. This will involve new structural framing, roofing, and finishes.

Skylights   Sometimes a nice feature to introduce into an attic is a skylight, or roof-window. Such windows provide considerable natural light, and perhaps even a view. Direct sunlight can also make the room extremely warm, however. You may wish to get an operable unit, which will allow ventilation, and therefore allow heat to escape. If the unit is very high, you can get a motorized unit. Skylights can also be specified with screens and shades.

Heating and Cooling Temperature control has to be analyzed on a case-by-case basis. Because climate, solar orientation, and construction vary so widely, there can be no rule of thumb.

Your options are to extend your existing system or to provide stand-alone units for the new space. Once you have decided where the office will be located, you can first speak with the company that services your existing system to see if it is practical to extend service to the new area.

An area that is normally cool in the summer months may become warm when additional lighting and equipment have been introduced. Hence, this area might now require additional cooling; this can be determined beforehand by a power analysis (see Chapter 4, Electrical Power Requirements). By adding a window air conditioning unit, you may inadvertently tip the electrical loading. An air conditioning unit should not be on the same circuit as any of your electronic equipment.

If you decide to introduce new heating or cooling into your office area, you should consider separate controls for energy conservation. You may want to put the office area on a setback thermostat.

Consider the effects on space and view before you introduce any new system. For instance, the addition of a baseboard radiator may reduce floor space; a window air conditioner may obscure the only view of the outside. In the latter case, a low-profile unit, or a unit mounted through the wall, can preserve your view.

Electrical There is a good chance that you will need some additional electrical circuits in your home office. You will almost certainly need additional outlets. This may be true even if you are simply planning to use existing space as an office. You should develop an electrical outlet plan that relates to the furniture and equipment you will be using, as well as their locations (see Chapters 4 and 5).

Plumbing   If you are planning to add a sink to your new office area, you will have to be concerned with the delivery of hot and cold water, the removal of waste water, and ventilation of the waste line (vent stack). Plumbing can affect other aspects of the house, because lines and stacks take up space and often require the opening of walls or ceilings. If your existing hot water heater is far away from the new sink location, you may want to consider putting in a smaller, separate hot water heater at the new location.

If you are planning to add a restroom, the wasteline for the commode is of a large diameter and is the most difficult line to run. As a rule, the closer you can position the new wet areas to existing water and waste lines, the less difficult and costly it will be to install them. If you are lucky enough to have more than one choice as to where you can locate your office within your home, existing water and waste line locations may help you to make the decision.

Additions   Additions require more forethought and planning than do renovations. This is because you are affecting land use and developing and adding space, which must be attached to the existing structure. By and large, the square foot cost of an addition is considerably higher than the cost of new freestanding construction of equal size.

Since the addition will add more building area to your land, and because setback requirements may prevent you from placing the addition in the location of choice, it is important to obtain preliminary approvals from the authorities, before proceeding with anything more than very preliminary site plan drawings.

Furthermore, you have to consider utility service to your house. If you have a septic system, there will be limitations on where you can place the addition. Power and water service to the house may be in the way of your proposed addition, which could cause additional expense or other complications.

Even though your house may have been surveyed when you bought it, the town will most likely require another survey as part of the required submission for a building permit, to be certain that you are in compliance with all setbacks and property and utility easements. The cost of surveys, and, indeed, even the cost of a building permit, are additional line item costs that should be identified and included in the project budget.

Time and Cost   Once you have a good understanding of the scope and project size, have chosen a suitable location, and have discussed the project with building officials, your next step is to estimate construction time and cost.

If your project is relatively simple, and if you feel that you can describe the work verbally, by a written list of work, by sketches, or by a combination of these methods, you may then want to meet with a general contractor, who can give you a rough estimate and time frame.

Professional Design Services   For complicated renovations, for an addition, or for a new home, you should at the outset consider hiring an architect, who can develop drawings and specifications for you. This route has a number of advantages:

1. Working with the design professional, you can discuss details in advance of construction. This is always better than having to make decisions while tradesmen are on the job, pressuring you to proceed.

2. A design professional can also help you to develop an independent cost estimate, which will serve as a basis of comparison when analyzing proposals from contractors.

3. The drawings are a standard basis of comparison, especially if you elect to get competitive bids from several contractors. It isn't helpful or fair to anyone to ask contractors to submit bids based on their individual interpretations of the project.

4. You have drawings to submit to the building department, which may be a requirement in your jurisdiction anyway.

5. There is some standard of expectation that the contractor will be obliged to meet during the course of construction.

This may sound like a design professional's sales pitch, and it is. But I'm not selling my services here—for practical purposes, you will need to hire a local individual, someone I probably don't even know. After 25 years in the business, I can tell you that the money you spend on an experienced professional will come back to you, in savings, over the course of the project. The end result will also be better.

Disruptions during Renovations or Additions

Perhaps the most disconcerting aspect of the construction process, from the owner's point of view, is the disruption to daily living that occurs during the course of renovation.

In most circumstances, the owner, or perhaps it is a family, chooses to remain in the home during construction. When construction begins, everyone is enthusiastic. As time wears on, the banging, noise, and layers of dust begin to accumulate in an unpleasant way. Occasionally, there are disruptions to electric and water services. Half way through the process, nerves typically get on edge.

Scheduling

If you can't move out of your house during construction, the next best thing is to develop a schedule prior to commencement, remembering that circumstances such as weather or delivery delays can get in the way of the best intentions.

Phasing

Sometimes a contractor can confine his work to one area, finish it, and go onto another area that you have vacated for the finished location. This "phasing" process usually extends the overall construction period, but it may be more suitable if you intend to remain in the house during construction.

A Summary of Advice

1. Do your homework. Initial planning will ultimately save you time, money and aggravation. Remember that planning a home office along with renovation or new construction is like having two jobs rolled into one.

2. Be certain to obtain the necessary approvals before you proceed.

3. Spend time carefully preparing a budget, and expect some cost overruns or contingencies. That's part of it all.

4. Life isn't perfect, and things don't always go according to plan. Maintain your cool, and work through a problem, rather than becoming part of the problem.

5. If you are planning a renovation that involves structural changes, or an addition, you would do well to involve the services of a licensed professional at the outset. Although it seems like an additional cost that buys no hard goods, it will undoubtedly save you money and time in the long run.

CHAPTER FOURTEEN
FINISHING WITH STYLE

PERHAPS THE BEST PART ABOUT HAVING a home office, is that you can have it "your way." The location, planning, furnishing style, colors, fabrics, art, plants, all are yours to choose.

The decorative aspects of interior design could fill another book, and many good ones have already been written. With respect to your personal freedom in this area, I am simply going to offer some general guidelines so that you can make your own decisions as you develop your personal work space.

Keeping Things Neat

Organization is the single most important aspect of office design. This extends to everything you have in your work space, including what you put on the walls, leave on the floor, or let hang around loose.

Wastepaper baskets and roll-around files are the only movable things that should be on the floor of your office. Stacks of paper, file boxes, and unused equipment should be stored away as quickly as possible, so as not to get in the way of your own efficient motion within your work space as well as your ability to locate things quickly. You also don't want to have to move one thing to get to another—it wastes time and energy.

If you are planning for an employee or two, it is important for them to feel comfortable. A well-organized and uncluttered space, where all occupants can get to everything easily, will add professionalism to your work zone and make others feel comfortable.

This is true for visitors as well. If they see a tidy, organized space, it will establish an element of trust and confidence.

Color
Colors that you choose for your office are, again, very personal. Hot or vibrant colors may be wearing on the eyes; dark colors may reduce ambient light.

In a work environment, the general rule is that you want fairly neutral, unobtrusive, and light colors. If you wish to add some pizzazz, you can do it with colorful art.

Decorative Finishes
Paint, wall coverings, paneling, flooring type, pattern, and color can dramatically enhance the comfort and aesthetic appeal of your work environment. All finishes should be considered together, working as a group. You may wish to seek some professional assistance in coordinating them. Design assistance may be available at the retail outlet where you will be purchasing materials, or through a design professional.

Lighting
Lighting can dramatically enhance the overall "feel" of a space, and is unfortunately often neglected by novice designers (see Chapter 11, Task Lighting). If you plan on a renovation or addition, you should have a discussion about lighting with your design professional early in the planning process.

Art
When thinking about what you put on the walls of your work space, keep it simple, and try to develop a common theme.

The theme may be appropriate to your particular business, or it may be something that is personally appealing to you, such as sailing or nature photos.

Your choices should be pleasing to the eye and set a general mood that will help you to stay relaxed.

Knickknacks and collectibles tend to get knocked over or in the way in an office and should be kept to a minimum, or displayed in such a way that they are out of the way and protected.

Plants/Interior Landscape   Plants add warmth and life to an office environment. The plastic variety, in my opinion, are more suitable for fast food chains than for offices.

If you do choose live plants, however, remember that they will need light and care. Clients don't take kindly to conferencing with you and a dead plant. What's worse, you may not notice the plant corpse, and the client may be too polite to alert you to it. So if you have plants in your office, remember to take good care of them.

Style   Some excellent examples of home office design, of varying complexity, style, and budgets, are to be found at the conclusion of this chapter. They may help you to develop a vision of your own home office, a vision that suits your work style, taste, and pocketbook.

Chapter 7, Workstation Furniture, also includes a broad variety of furniture styles for varying tastes and budgets.

Whether you are building a brand new home on a magnificent site or creating space in the corner of a bedroom, it is important to select a style that suits your personality as well as your type of business.

Pleasure   You should derive pleasure from the organization and decor of your home office. Not only do you deserve it, but it will indirectly affect your mood and the quality of your work.

Figure 14-1
A home office version of the corner office, designed by Alexandria Lanuk, ASID. Although this is a standard desk-credenza arrangement, electronic equipment, including a notebook computer and fax machine, are nicely integrated into a very personal space. Amid traditional icons, notice the high intensity lighting and the Aeron™ ergonomic task chair by Herman Miller.
Courtesy of ATL Interiors, Stamford, CT. Photo by Tim Lee Photography.

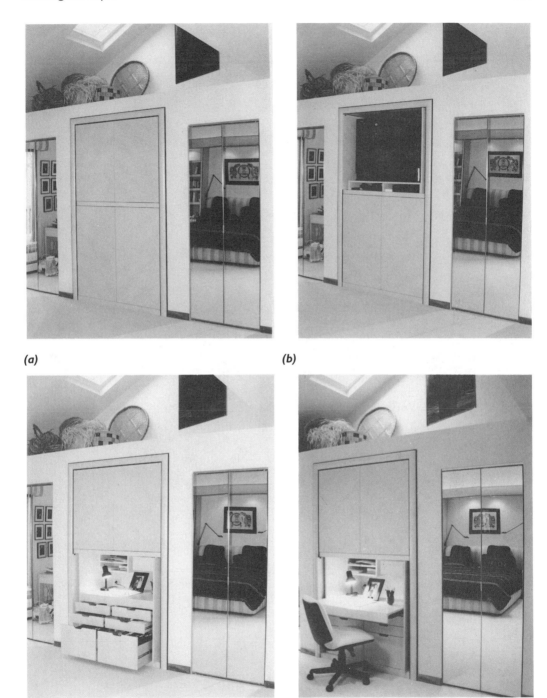

(a) *(b)*

(c) *(d)*

Figure 14-2 (a) through (d)
Fine example of a versatile, custom designed office in a closet, which also includes storage and entertainment features. Doors open and slide into pockets, out of the way. When the doors are closed, the office is out of view.
Courtesy of Pat Valentine Ziv ASID, PVZ Space Plan & Design, Ridgewood, NJ.

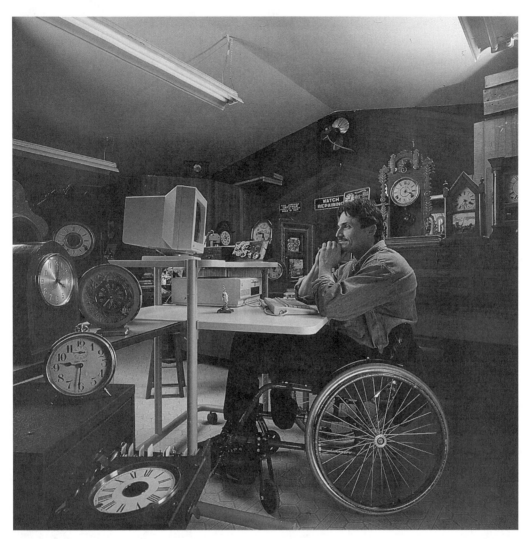

Figure 14-3
An example of a theme environment developed around a working home office.

Courtesy of Anthro Corporation, Tualatin OR.

Figure 14-4
This very sleek and well-organized home office, designed by Sandra Johnson, ASID, for a professional couple, needs to serve as a writing and conference area, as well as providing space for their shared home records. One of them is collaborating on a textbook with other professors, who meet frequently in the office. Aesthetically, the office has finish materials that blend with the master bedroom adjacent to it. Lighting is extremely important, so a low voltage cable system with small intense fixtures was used. The fixtures may then be placed exactly where needed.

Courtesy of Sandra Johnson, ASID, SK Johnson Design, Aspen, CO.

Figure 14-5
This home office was a former library within a stately Victorian in Warrington, PA, which required
extensive refurbishing. Designed by Audrey Long, ASID Allied, for a female author, family
photographs and drafts of manuscripts were positioned in various locations throughout the room.
Furnishings were selected to imply a working, but relaxed environment; a visitor is meant to feel
welcome and comfortable amid the archives of volumes needed for research purposes.
Courtesy of Audrey Long Interior Design, New Hope, PA. Photo by Bill Blizzard Photography .

Figure 14-6
This photo demonstrates how all the needs of a home office, including aesthetic ones, may be satisfied through the selections available from one integrated RTA panel system.
Courtesy of 3K Möbel, Irvine, CA. .

Figure 14-7
The suggestion of serious decision-making radiates from the oval form, which provides the primary work space and study for an attorney's home office, designed by the office of Barry Berkus, AIA, of B³ Architects + Planners. The walls of the room's circumference are filled with reference books and art. The desk and cabinetry feature a work platform with retractable keyboard, and an electronic spine for computer and telecommunications. Utilizing outside secretarial and related services, remote connections from the outside world network to this private space in a seamless manner, creating a fully operating law firm at home.
Courtesy of Barry Berkus, AIA, B³ Architects + Planners, Santa Barbara, CA. Photo by Dugan/Powers/Yocum, Photographers.

Figure 14-8
Exterior view of the residence that contains the "oval office."
Courtesy of Barry Berkus, AIA, B³ Architects + Planners, Santa Barbara, CA. Photo by Dugan/Powers/Yocum, Photographers .

Figure 14-9
This office design solution, by architect Patricia Motzkin, AIA, utilizes space in a hallway in a stately San Francisco Victorian home. Custom cherrywood casework is organized along both sides of the hall. One side is designed for fax and copier; the other side accommodates three work stations. The overall effect of the office is quite traditional, but its functional ease is entirely contemporary.
Courtesy of Patricia Motzkin, AIA, Patricia Motzkin Architecture, Berkeley, CA.

Figure 14-10
Exterior view of the house that contains the office shown above.
Courtesy of Patricia Motzkin, AIA, Patricia Motzkin Architecture,

Figure 14-11
**Architect Carol Kurth, AIA, created this home-office in "attic" space over a garage, an office that
is nothing less than first class all the way. Soaring interior roof planes and a grand palladian
window behind the main work area enhance drama of the attic location. Cohesive treatment of
structural columns, flooring, and lighting design make this a one-of-a-kind home office environment.**
Courtesy of Kurth & Kurth Architects/Carol Kurth, AIA, Bedford, NY. Photo © by Peter Mauss / Esto.

Figure 14-12
Exterior view. Note the palladian window centered over the garage, where the home office is located.
Courtesy of Kurth & Kurth Architects, Bedford, NY. Photo © by Peter Mauss / Esto.

CHAPTER FIFTEEN
CONCLUSION

IT'S ONE OF THOSE COLD, GRAY, NEW ENGLAND Sunday afternoons in November. We just finished raking leaves in our back yard, trying to beat the threatening snow. I'm now sitting in my own home office, doing a little weekend work, and thinking about lighting a fire in the living room fireplace adjacent to my work space. I'm also thinking about how remarkably cozy the days are—that is the mid-week and weekend days—and how quickly they are passing by. There's certainly a convenience and a sense of calm about working at home.

One thing is for sure—more and more of us are going to have the opportunity to try this lifestyle on for size, whether it is part-time or full-time, self-elected or otherwise. Although I have stayed primarily within the boundaries of my expertise, which is the physical planning of a home work environment, there are also psychological, social, and business aspects, all of which are critical to work-at-home success.

Feelings of isolation, lack of motivation and personal discipline are among the most commonly reported problems associated with working at home. There are several books currently on the market that may help you cope with these challenges. If working at home is new or experimental for you, one of these books will definitely be worthwhile reading. Nothing paves the way for success better than being well-informed.

Nevertheless, all these books stress the importance of a tidy, well-planned and properly equipped work environment. When you get your personal work space physically organized in a way that is efficient for you and pleasing to you, it will surely be a life raft of sustenance and comfort for you, just as mine is for me. I hope I will have helped you to get there—good luck!

DIRECTORY OF CONTRIBUTORS

The following consultants, manufacturers, and retail establishments contributed material, advice, drawings, charts, and photographs for inclusion in this book.

Art Consultants

Jacqueline Hamilton, Art Consultant
P.O. Box 1483
Houston, TX 77251-1483
713.465.8890

Business Consultants

Joanne H. Pratt Associates
3520 Routh Street
Dallas, TX 75219
214.528.6540

CADD Programs

Abracadata
P.O. Box 2440
Eugene, OR 97402
800.451.4871

Design Professionals

Adaptive Architecture
112 Great Oaks Office Park
Albany, NY 12203
518.464.6232

ATL Interiors
433 Den Road
Stamford, CT 06903
203.322.2263

B³Architecture + Planning
223 E. De La Guerra Street
Santa Barbara, CA 93101-2248
805.966.1547

Bianco Giolitto Architects
500 Plaza Middlesex
Middletown, CT 06457
860.344.9332

Robert T. Coolidge, Architect
800 Village Walk #267
Guilford, CT 06437
203.458.9759

Roger Gohl Design
2643 Stoner Avenue
Los Angeles, CA 90064
310.479.0754

SK Johnson Design
215 S. Monarch G103
Aspen, CO 81611
970.925.6191

Kuegler Associates Engineers
203 Kendall Road
Tewksbury, MA 01876
508.640.1794

Office of Carol Kurth, Architect
Arcade Building
Bedford, NY 10506-0323
914.234.2595

Audrey Long Interior Design
105 Chapel Road
New Hope, PA 18938
215.862.2263

Magnusson Architects
853 Broadway, Suite 809
New York, NY 10003
212.293.6333

Patricia Motzkin Architecture
2927 Newbury Street
Berkeley, CA 94703
510.649.7708

PVZ Space Plan & Design
560 Grove Street
Ridgewood, NJ 07450
201.612.9246

Desktop Video

PictureTel Corporation
222 Roswood Drive
Danvers, MA 01923
508.762.5178

Target Technologies, Inc.
6714 Netherlands Drive
Wilmington, NC 28405
910.395.6100

Ergonomic Tools

Balt, Inc.
201 N. Crockett
Cameron, TX 76520
800.749.2258

The Container Store
2000 Valwood Parkway
Dallas, TX 75234-8800
800.733.3532

Details! Inc.
6100 E. Paris Avenue
Caledonia, MI 49316
800.833.0411

Ergonomic Logic, Inc.
205 Vista Boulevard, #101
Sparks, NV 89434
800.527.6600

Flex-Y-Plan, Inc.
6960 W. Ridge Road
Fairview, PA 16415-0829
800.458.0552

Hold Everything
100 N. Point Street
San Francisco, CA 94133
800.421.2264

Kinesis Corporation
22232 17th Avenue, S.E.
Bothell, Wa 98021
800.454.6374

The Knoll Group
105 Wooster Street
New York, NY 10012
800.445.5045

Information Resources

**American Association
of Home Based Businesses**
P.O. Box 10023
Rockville, MD 20849
202.310.3130

American Institute of Architects
1735 New York Avenue, N.W.
Washington, D.C. 20006
202.626.7300

American Society of Interior Designers
608 Massachusetts Avenue, S.E.
Washington, D.C. 2002
202.546.3480

Business Products Industry Association
3201 N. Fairfax Street
Alexandria, VA 22314-2696
800.542.6672

Ergometrix
2439 Walgrove Avenue
Los Angeles, CA 90066
800.429.9965

Mail Order

The Container Store
2000 Valwood Parkway
Dallas, TX 75234-8800
800.733.3532

Mail Order

Hold Everything
100 N. Point Street
San Francisco, CA 94133
800.421.2264

Retail Outlets

The Container Store
2000 Valwood Parkway
Dallas, TX 75234-8800
800.733.3532

Hold Everything
100 N. Point Street
San Francisco, CA 94133
800.421.2264

The Home Depot
2727 Paces Ferry Road
Atlanta, GA 30339
770.433.8211

Staples
100 Pennsylvania Avenue
Framingham, MA 01701
800.333.3024

Seating

Alma Group
2400 Sterling Avenue
Elkhart, IN 46516
219.293.0621

Global Group
17 W. Stowe Road
Marlton, NJ 08053
800.220.1900

Haworth, Inc.
One Haworth Center
Holland, MI 49423-9576
800.344.2600

Herman Miller for the Home
855 E. Main Avenue
Zeeland, MI 49464-0302
800.646.4400

The Knoll Group
105 Wooster Street
New York, NY 10012
800.445.5045

LA Z BOY Business Furniture
1284 N. Telegraph Road
Monroe, MI 48162
313.241.2105

Turnstone
3528 Lousma Drive, S.E.
Wyoming, MI 49548-2251
800.887.6786

ZackBack International, Inc.
P.O. Box 9100
Rochester, MN 55903
800.748.8464

Storage/Filing

3K Möbel
16641 Hale Avenue
Irvine, CA 92714-5048
714.474.0100

Details! Inc.
6100 E. Paris Avenue
Caledonia, MI 49316
800.833.0411

Global Group
17 W. Stowe Road
Marlton, NJ 08053
800.220.1900

Hold Everything
100 N. Point Street
San Francisco, CA 94133
800.421.2264

HON
Storage Systems
Muscatine, IA 52671
319.264.7022

Task Lighting

Details! Inc.
6100 E. Paris Avenue
Caledonia, MI 49316
800.833.0411

Waldmann Lighting
9 W. Century Drive
Wheeling, IL 60090
800.634.0007

Workstations

3K Möbel
16641 Hale Avenue
Irvine, CA 92714-5048
714.474.0100

Alma Group
2400 Sterling Avenue
Elkhart, IN 46516
219.293.0621

Anthro Corporation
10450 S.W. Manhasset Drive
Tualatin, OR 97062
800.325.3841

Balt, Inc.
201 N. Crockett
Cameron, TX 76520
800.749.2258

The Container Store
2000 Valwood Parkway
Dallas, TX 75234-8800
800.733.3532

Global Group
17 W. Stowe Road
Marlton, NJ 08053
800.220.1900

Haworth, Inc.
One Haworth Center
Holland, MI 49423-9576
800.344.2600

Herman Miller for the Home
855 E. Main Avenue
Zeeland, MI 49464-0302
800.646.4400

Hooker Furniture Corp.
P.O. Box 4708
Martinsville, VA 24115
703.632.2133

LA Z BOY Business Furniture
1284 N. Telegraph Road
Monroe, MI 48162
313.241.2105

Nucraft
5151 W. River Drive
Comstock Park, MI 49321
616.784.6016

O'Sullivan Industries
1900 Gulf Street
Lamar, MO 64759
417.682.3322

Peter Pepper Products
17929 S. Susana Road
Compton, CA 90024
310.639.0390

Sauder Woodworking
502 Middle Street
Archbold, OH
800.537.8560

Sligh Furniture Company
1201 Industrial Avenue
Holland, MI 49423
616.392.7101

Steelcase
901 44th Street S.E.
Grand Rapids, MI 49508
800.227.2960

Turnstone
3528 Lousma Drive, S.E.
Wyoming, MI 49548-2251
800.887.6786

INDEX